Introduction to
Integrational Linguistics

Related Pergamon books

FIGUEROA	Sociolinguistic Metatheory
HARRE & HARRIS	Linguistics and Philosophy
HARRIS & WOLF	Integrational Linguistics: A First Reader
KOERNER & ASHER	Concise History of the Language Sciences
KOMATSU & HARRIS	Saussure's Third Course of Lectures on General Linguistics (1910-1911)
KOMATSU & WOLF	Saussure's Second Course of Lectures on General Linguistics (1908-1909)
KOMATSU & WOLF	Saussure's First Course of Lectures on General Linguistics (1907)

Related journals

Journal of Pragmatics
Editor: Jacob Mey

Language & Communication
Editors: Roy Harris and Talbot J. Taylor

Language Sciences
Editor: Nigel Love

Lingua
Editors: Teun Hoekstra, John Anderson and Neil Smith

Free specimen copies of journals available on request

Language & Communication Library

This series features books and edited collections of papers which focus attention on key theoretical issues concerning language and other forms of communication. The history of these issues and their cultural implications also fall within its scope, as do radical proposals for new approaches in linguistics and communication studies. The series has already published important contributions to critical debate both by younger writers and by established scholars, and welcomes more. Inquiries from potential contributors should be addressed to the Series Editor, Roy Harris.

Introduction to Integrational Linguistics

ROY HARRIS

Oxford, England

Pergamon

An imprint of Elsevier Science

ELSEVIER SCIENCE Ltd
The Boulevard, Langford Lane
Kidlington, Oxford OX5 1GB, UK

Library of Congress Cataloging-in-Publication Data

Harris, Roy, 1931-
    Introduction to integrational linguistics
        / by Roy Harris. -- 1st ed.
        p.   cm. -- (Language and communication library
    series)
    A companion volume to Integrational linguistics :
a first reader
    Includes bibliographical references and index.
    ISBN 0-08-043364-2 (hardcover : alk. paper)
    1. Linguistics.   I. Title.   II. Series: Language &
communication library.
    P121.H33   1998
    410--dc21
                                          98-34395
                                             CIP

British Library Cataloguing in Publication Data
A catalogue record from the British Library has been applied for.

First edition 1998

ISBN: 0 08 043364 2

∞ The paper used in this publication meets the requirements of
ANSI/NISO Z39.48-1992
(Permanence of Paper).

Printed in The Netherlands.

Contents

Preface   ix

1   Language and Communication   1

   The orthodox view   2
   Languages presuppose communication   5
   Modern linguistics   7
   Integrational linguistics   9
   Segregationism   9
   Theoretical compromises   13
   Linguistics and the linguist   15
   Linguistics as hocus-pocus   16
   The conditions of linguistic inquiry   18
   The sender-receiver model of communication   20
   The missing context   22
   Linguistic 'observation'   23
   Linguistic reflexivity   24
   Reflexive and non-reflexive communication   27
   Communication as integration   28

2   Language and the Language Myth   31

   The history of the language myth   31
   Modern versions of the language myth   34
   Integrational linguistics and demythologization   38
   Languages in history   42
   The dialect myth   44
   The myth of 'standard' languages   46

	The idiolect myth	48
	The status of 'languages'	50
	The myth of the 'native speaker'	52
	Languages and linguistic behaviour	53
	Reintegrating languages	55
	Linguistic idealizations	60
3	**Language and Meaning**	**63**
	Meanings as concepts	63
	Semantics and 'mental reality'	64
	The metalanguage of semantics	65
	Meaning and truth	66
	Semantic determinacy	68
	Meanings and intentions	70
	Stipulative definition	72
	Demythologizing semantics	73
	Integrational semantics	76
	Semantics and literacy	77
	Shoring up the fixed code	80
	Making meaning	81
	Semantic indeterminacy	84
	The semantics of lexicography	85
	Regulating meanings	88
	Metaphor	89
	Meaning as doing	91
4	**Language and Discourse**	**93**
	Discourse and context	93
	Theories of context	95
	Contextualization and cotemporality	98
	Contextualization and reflexivity	100
	Text and context	102
	Context and understanding	105
5	**Language and Writing**	**109**
	Writing and linguistics	110
	Writing and speech	111
	Writing as integration	115
	The writing process	117
	Writing and space	120
	Defining writing	121
	Writing and codification	123

6   Language and Society   125

Are linguistic facts social facts?   126
Social facts and psychological reality   128
Linguistic variation revisited   130
A new start   131
Linguistic communities and linguistic determinacy   132
Society and the 'limits' of language   134
Deixis as contextual (in)determinacy   136
Cotemporality and linguistic facts   140
Axioms of integrational semiology   144
A'lay-oriented' linguistics   145

Postscript   149

References   151

Index   157

Preface

Integrationists take a radically different view of language and communication from that held by most twentieth-century theorists. In so doing integrationists offer, both implicitly and explicitly, a critique of the orthodox thinking which still shapes many university courses in linguistics, psycholinguistics, communication studies and allied subjects. Whether or not one accepts the integrationist critique, examining its claims provides a useful way of putting the orthodoxy in perspective. Even if familiarity with integrationist principles serves no other purpose, it is likely to sharpen an awareness of the problems that are involved in attempting to answer seemingly simple questions about how one person is able to communicate with another.

Students of language and communication will find that an integrational approach is of relevance to many matters that are of direct interest to them. These include the identification of words and meanings, the analysis of linguistic structure, the description of languages, the status of grammatical rules, translation, the relations between speech and writing, the interpretation of literary texts, the establishment of language standards, dialectology, language-teaching, and the role of authority and power in communication processes. But this book does not attempt to cover this very wide range of topics. Instead, it focuses on presenting as clearly and concisely as possible the theoretical basis of integrationism. Grasping this basis is an essential prerequisite for applying integrationism to any specific set of problems.

The presentation assumes only a minimal acquaintance with the technicalities of linguistics or any other university discipline, but some familiarity with the main currents of modern thought. It attempts to state, in a succinct and accessible form, the main tenets of integrational linguistics and to explain how these differ from those held by the majority of contemporary language theorists. It nevertheless tries to avoid becoming a mere catalogue of points, and challenges the reader to engage with the controversial issues in question. In this respect it is perhaps more provocative than introductory textbooks are usually expected to be. A select bibliography of integrationist publications is also included.

The text is a revised version of lectures to students given by the author as Distinguished Visiting Professor at the University of Adelaide in spring 1997. I should like here to thank colleagues at Adelaide and Professor Peter Mühlhäusler in particular for that opportunity.

R.H.

1

Language and Communication

Integrationism proposes a view of human communication in general. **Integrational linguistics** is the application of integrationism to the specific case of language. The aim of integrational linguistics is to change the way people think about language.

That aim sets integrational linguistics apart from most other current approaches to language study, which either claim to be neutral with respect to such questions, or else tend to assume that the 'right' way to think about language is already exemplified in the modern discipline of linguistics.

T.H. Huxley once observed that it is 'the customary fate of new truths to begin as heresies and to end as superstitions'. Integrationism is still at the heresy stage. Which means that most of its intellectual energies are still directed towards challenging an orthodoxy already established.

Setting out to change the way people think about language is an ambitious project: certainly no less ambitious than trying to change the way people think about war, or health, or sexual relations, or (as in Huxley's case) biology. Perhaps even more ambitious than any of these, since language is involved in all of them and in many more human concerns as well.

If you say you want to change the way people think about something, this implies that in your view there is something not good about their current thinking. It does not necessarily mean you believe that all their thinking on the subject is utterly wrong. It is in fact usual for heresies to take over a great deal of the orthodoxy they oppose. But wanting to change a way of thinking does suggest there is something inadequate or awry about it. So you automatically incur an obligation to explain what is defective or undesirable about the thing you want to change. The immediately following subsection is a preliminary attempt to discharge this obligation. To get a fuller picture, it will be necessary to read the rest of this book.

The orthodox view

Linguistics is commonly presented as an 'objective' investigation (often called a 'science') of language and languages. We are invited to see linguistics as investigating language(s) in much the same way as chemistry investigates chemical phenomena, geology investigates geological phenomena, or history investigates historical events. Thus we encounter such claims as the following:

> Linguistics performs at least two tasks: it is concerned with the study of particular languages as ends in themselves, in order to be able to produce complete and accurate descriptions of them; and it also studies languages as a means to a further end, in order to be able to obtain information about the nature of language in general. Linguists are thus those who want to find out how language 'works', and they do this through the study of specific languages. They try to be as objective as possible... Put simply, Linguistics is the scientific way of studying language – or perhaps it should be Language, to emphasize the fact that we mean both language in general as well as languages in particular. (Crystal, 1985, pp.24-5)

This is the orthodox view of what students of linguistics are being invited to engage in. Integrational linguistics extends no such invitation, for the simple reason that the above invitation reflects the very way of thinking that integrationists would like to see changed. The invitation the integrationist would like to extend to students is, by contrast, one to engage in the first instance in critical reflection on claims such as this.

If we examine the above passage, it is evident that from the start a number of quite important assumptions are already being taken for granted; and the integrationist would say that, far from reflecting any 'objective' or 'scientific' stance, these assumptions are highly controversial. The first and most far-reaching concerns the relationship between two objects of inquiry, one identified by the term 'language' and the other by the term 'languages'. What exactly the relationship is remains unspecified, but the fairly clear implication seems to be that by studying the latter we can obtain information about the former. In other words, 'languages' (when fully and accurately described) provide evidence about 'language'. Indeed, this order of proceeding is presented as a defining characteristic of linguistics.

The priorities thus implied beg a number of important questions. For what is far from clear, precisely, is how 'languages' relate to 'language'. It would be naive to assume that English, French, Latin, etc. stand to 'language' as do oak, ash, elm, etc. to 'tree'. So why not, it might be asked, start at the other end with the study of 'language', and leave English, French, Latin, etc. for later? This would at least avoid the problem of deciding how many languages had to be studied before the linguist could be sure of having amassed enough evidence to draw reliable conclusions.

One objection to tackling 'language' first might be that 'language' is not available for direct examination. And something like this seems to be implied by the insistence in orthodox linguistics that it is the study of 'languages' that provides the proper (or perhaps the only?) way into the study of 'language'. This order of priority in fact echoes the historical growth of European linguistics (see further discussion below), but that is not the reason usually given in justification of the claim that 'languages' provide 'evidence' about 'language'. The usual reason is to say that 'language' is a human 'faculty', with the implication that faculties cannot be studied except inductively through the examination of what they enable human beings to do.

Thus we find claims such as the following:

> The linguist [...] studies languages, his own and foreign languages, as examples of mankind's faculty of language, to learn more about the way language works and how it may best be described and analysed. (Robins, 1971, p.15)

A 'faculty' was traditionally supposed to be a 'power of the mind' responsible for certain mental feats that human beings could perform. Now this might be acceptable as a basis for linguistics if it were clear that there was such a thing as 'the language faculty' and that 'languages' were the products for which this faculty was directly and solely responsible. But this, an integrationist will point out, seems highly questionable.

On the contrary, linguistic communication appears to involve the integration of very diverse abilities, and the integration is so complex that it becomes problematic to identify or single out what exactly is 'linguistic' in it. So, far from being uncontroversially 'given' as an ultimate object of inquiry, 'language' turns out to be a theoretical postulate which has the main function of providing a hypothetical source for 'languages', or a classification under which the study of many different 'languages' can be grouped. In other words, it looks suspiciously as if the underlying rationale is exactly the opposite of what the orthodox apologia claims: 'the language faculty' is an abstraction tailor-made to accommodate, justify and collect together the study of 'languages'.

But there is worse to follow. What the orthodox linguist calls 'languages' are not uncontroversially 'given' objects of inquiry either. Again, on the contrary, what belongs or does not belong to some particular language, who exactly its speakers are, and who has the right to determine such matters are questions that have often triggered not only debate but actions and attitudes of a kind that no human community should be proud of (although some clearly are). Whether 'the language' you speak (or claim to speak) is X or Y may well be a substantive issue in deciding whether you are a candidate for expropriation, deportation or extermination. And these are more urgent linguistic matters than, for instance, deciding how many parts of speech there are. The assumption that professional linguists can get involved with the latter but somehow stand 'objectively' or 'scientifically' outside the former is not only an arrogant idea but a dangerous one.

The way people think about language is at the heart not only of many social and political issues but of their view of their own cultural identity and of their relations with other members of what they take to be 'their' community or communities. To treat these matters as marginal or 'non-linguistic' (in order to focus linguistic inquiry elsewhere) is *already* to promote a certain way of thinking about language. It is misleading to present linguistics to students as fitting naturally into some unquestionable and tested model of inquiry established in advance, and to proclaim it as the 'scientific' way of looking at language. That is the impression academic linguists often like to give of their subject, but it is not how integrationists view it.

Thinking of language in the way described above begs all kinds of questions about people's understanding of their own linguistic responsibilities, of their own linguistic creativity, of their social relationships with others, and of their community's relationships with other communities. For the integrationist, these are good enough reasons for trying to develop an alternative conceptual framework for linguistic inquiry.

The point of departure, in an integrationist perspective, is not the existence of complex cultural objects called 'languages' but, simply, the attempts by human beings to integrate whatever they are capable of doing into the various activity patterns we call 'communication'. That – if anything – is what is 'given'; and it is 'given' in experience to every one of us, long before we have any grasp of the slippery and tortuous notion of what 'a language' is, or how many of them there are, or whether 'ours' is different from anyone else's.

Languages presuppose communication

It is an important tenet of integrationism that unless we understand the processes of *communication* then we shall end up with no more than a partial and distorted view of language(s). Communication, in other words, is not a secondary purpose that just happens to be served by language. (As, for example, artificial lighting is just one of the purposes that happens to be served by electricity. Electricity could still serve human needs even if human beings could see perfectly well in the dark and therefore did not need it for illumination.) On the contrary, for the integrationist, language cannot be divorced from communication. Without the spur provided by human communicational needs, *Homo sapiens* would still be a languageless species. Furthermore, if human beings suddenly ceased communicating with one another, language too would cease. Language and communication are intrinsically – and not merely adventitiously – related.

For the integrationist, we are starting from the wrong end if we suppose that linguistic communication presupposes languages. The right theoretical priority is exactly the reverse: **languages presuppose communication**.

So this provides another reason for questioning the orthodox view which starts from a postulated relationship between a human faculty ('language') and its alleged cultural products ('languages'). For nothing in that relationship suggests that there may be some altogether wider field of inquiry within which the study of language(s) needs to be situated. Insofar as linguistics acknowledges that linguistic communication is only one form of communication among many, that is merely paying lip-service to the superordinate category of 'communication'. It does not result in proposing in practice a different starting-point for the linguist's investigations. And one reason for this is that the professional linguist in any case adopts a very simplistic – and convenient – notion of what 'communication' is. That simplistic notion is another feature of the thinking about language that integrationists would like to see changed.

Communication, for the integrationist, is a much more complex matter than can be dealt with by saying that it requires the successful transmission of some message (*M*) from one individual to another. For this merely sets up another theoretical entity with dubious credentials (namely, 'the message') and endows it with the property of transmissibility. Even more dubious is the linguist's ready identification of the message with some form of words ('Come at once!', 'Attention à la marche!', etc.): once this is done, the linguist is back on safe linguistic terrain, and any problems of communication as such drop out of sight. (For anyone who does not 'get the message' clearly does not understand 'the language'.)

All these evasions are part and parcel of a way of thinking about language that is exemplified in a particularly explicit form in the theories and methodology of modern linguistics. That is why, for the integrationist, modern linguistics is worth studying (i.e. not to find out about 'language' but to see a clear example of a certain paradigm of thinking about it).

However, it would be misleading to suggest that modern linguistics is the only forum for the thinking about language that an integrationist wants to change. Here is an example from a recent Oxford University Press book with the ambitious title *Smart Thinking. Skills for Critical Understanding and Writing*, which purports to give students an introduction to 'informal logic'. The section entitled 'Understanding Language' tells the reader:

> There are four distinct 'levels' of language-use that build together to create 'language' as we know it. The first level is a *word* – for example, 'student' or 'reasoning' – which is the basic unit of language. When we put some words together, we get the second level: a *statement*, such as 'there are 200 students doing Applied Reasoning' [...] The third level of language-use is the *text*, which is made up of any group of statements, such as the sentence above [...] Finally, the last level of language-use is the *context*, which consists of all the elements outside a particular text that make it meaningful. (Allen, 1997, p. 10)

Doubtless there are many linguists who would throw up their hands in horror at the disconcerting crudity of such an account (which it might otherwise be supposed an integrationist had invented for purposes of parody); but the evidence shows that this way of thinking about language is basically no different from the orthodox linguist's. Language-use is presented as a matter of stringing units together, the allowable units and their combinations as being already available in advance for that operation, the combined whole then being slotted into some external environment or situation. This, according to the author of the above passage, is language 'as we know it'. *But it isn't.* It is an analysis imposed on language by adopting one narrow and rather questionable perspective.

Many more examples of this perspective could be cited. The point is mentioned here for two reasons. One is to demonstrate that this way of thinking about language is not a spectre conjured up by the integrationist but is actually being taught – today – quite explicitly as an ingredient of educational programmes. The other is in order to avoid giving the impression that integrationism is just about remote theoretical issues internal to the rather prickly and arcane discipline of linguistics. Having said that, however, it must be admitted that the 'questionable perspective' is nowhere more clearly exemplified and documented than in the history of modern linguistics.

Modern linguistics

Modern linguistics did not suddenly drop into the cultural landscape out of a clear blue sky. Its origins lie quite specifically in one academic tradition, the European grammatical tradition. Grammar was one of the 'liberal arts', taught by specialists and for centuries an important component in school and university studies. It was not until the nineteenth century that 'linguistics' emerged under that name and was recognized as a field of scholarly inquiry distinct from neighbouring fields.

This was essentially a question of academic politics. Those who wanted linguistics to be a separate discipline insisted first of all on a difference between 'philology' and 'linguistics'. The public rationale for doing so appealed to a popular nineteenth-century distinction between historical sciences and natural sciences. What was claimed was that whereas philology belonged to the historical sciences, linguistics belonged to the natural sciences. (It was a kind of botany in the domain of language.) This was the view championed by a number of nineteenth-century authorities, including Schleicher, Max Müller and Hovelacque. Others, for example Bréal, disagreed. Bréal called treating linguistics as a natural science 'a clever political act' (Bréal, 1897, p.279). In this he was undoubtedly right.

There were in any case serious problems about setting up 'linguistics' on this basis. One was that many people could not see much difference between linguistics and what was then called 'comparative philology'. The most prominent practitioners of linguistics turned out to be also comparative philologists. So on the purely terminological level the distinction was difficult to maintain. Another difficulty was that although a case could be made out for treating phonetics as a natural science, since it fitted in under the physiological study of the human vocal tract, it was by no means so clear how morphology, syntax and semantics could be accommodated in this way. (How, for instance, did one apply the methods of the natural sciences to the analysis of meaning?) There was also a third problem. Most of the advances in the study of languages during the nineteenth century had been made by elucidating past developments in the various Indo-European languages. So it was awkward to maintain that linguistics did not belong with the historical sciences.

In the end a compromise was reached, largely due to the theoretical astuteness of Ferdinand de Saussure (1857-1913), the scholar widely regarded as the founder of modern linguistics. Whether that compromise was ever valid is another question. But what matters more for our present purposes is that the academic continuity between European grammar and modern linguistics explains many things which would otherwise be inexplicable. In particular, it explains much of what linguists always tended to take for granted about the way language 'works'. For the pioneers of modern linguistics were themselves graduates of an educational system in which language had been made to 'work' in a particular way: it was a system into which the traditional teachings of the grammarians had been incorporated at a very basic level. In short, 'linguistics' was never a radical break with the past, in spite of many claims to the contrary.

The traditional grammar on which modern linguistics was founded had originally been a programme designed for the teaching of Greek and Latin. This continues to be reflected in various ways right down to the present day. It is significant that although traditional grammar has often been criticized or even held up to ridicule by twentieth-century linguists, nevertheless modern linguistics has always retained, with modifications, a nucleus of basic concepts and distinctions that were already familiar to pupils in the schools of Greece and Rome. These include such notions as 'noun', 'verb', and other 'parts of speech'; 'conjugations' and 'declensions'; the division of 'sentences' into 'subject' and 'predicate'; 'rules' of 'agreement'; and, most important of all, the assumption that speech is composed of a succession of individual sounds corresponding to the letters of the alphabet.

As the term *grammar* already suggests, its basis was the study of the writing systems (Greek *grammata*, 'letters') that Greek and Roman children were taught. The historical accident that Greek and Latin were written alphabetically is the single factor which, perhaps more than any other, was to determine the way in which, many hundreds of years later, modern linguistics would develop. Both phonetics and phonology were to be based on the assumption that spoken languages could all be analysed into segmental units that corresponded to the vowel and consonant letters of the alphabet (or some extended version of the alphabet). If Greek, Latin and other European languages had traditionally been written in a non-alphabetic script, this assumption in all probability would never have been made.

These major debts to traditional European grammar, still evident after the passage of some two thousand years, are aptly summed up in the observation that the linguist is constantly 'working with concepts originally introduced by the grammarians' (Saussure, 1922, p.153). Although this remark dates from the early years of the present century, it remains true of the various schools and movements (structuralist, functionalist, systemic, generativist, etc.) that between them have since contributed to the establishment of mainstream modern linguistics. With the marginal exception of Sanskrit grammar (discovered by European scholars at the end of the eighteenth century) no other historical tradition has provided any significant conceptual input to linguistics as we know it today.

Integrational linguistics

It is against this background that one must situate the emergence of integrational linguistics during the past two decades. The term itself was first introduced (Harris, 1981a, p.165) to designate an approach to linguistic inquiry which would examine language from a different theoretical perspective from that adopted in the Western grammatical tradition and its modern linguistic continuations.

Since that original proposal, papers sympathetic in varying degrees to the integrational approach and critical of mainstream linguistics have been published in the journals *Language & Communication* and *Language Sciences*, and also in two independent volumes: *Redefining Linguistics* (ed. H.G. Davis and T.J. Taylor, London, Routledge, 1990) and *New Perspectives in Linguistics* (ed. G. Wolf, New York, Garland, 1992). The International Congress of Linguists has included panel sessions on integrational linguistics at the XVth world congress (Quebec 1992) and the XVIth (Paris 1997).

Two recent books that explore the integrational approach in greater depth than this one are:

- M. Toolan, *Total Speech. An Integrational Linguistic Approach to Language*, Durham, NC, Duke University Press, 1996.

- R. Harris, *Signs, Language and Communication. Integrational and Segregational Approaches*, London, Routledge, 1996.

A representative collection of integrationist papers on a variety of topics is:

- R. Harris and G. Wolf (Eds), *Integrational Linguistics: A First Reader*, Oxford, Pergamon, 1998.

Segregationism

The central criticism that the integrationist levels against mainstream modern linguistics runs as follows. Modern linguistics misrepresents the relationship between language and communication, and in so doing misrepresents language. This misrepresentation has its roots in certain assumptions that the linguist commonly makes about our everyday linguistic activities. These assumptions collectively identify a position which the integrationist calls **'segregationism'**.

The term alludes to the notion that linguistic and non-linguistic phenomena constitute two academically segregated domains of inquiry, and that within the former a domain pertaining to languages is to be segregated from the rest. The study of languages thus has its own autonomy within the study of language, its own methodology and programme(s) of research. It is supposedly independent of neighbouring domains; in particular, of the study of communication (to which it may contribute but on which it in no way relies).

The integrationist, on the other hand, holds that a theory of language(s) without a theory of communication is vacuous. For the primary manifestation of language is in that gamut of human abilities that are brought into play in the processes of verbal communication. There is no autonomy for linguistics, because we cannot in practice segregate linguistic knowledge from extra-linguistic knowledge. The two domains are integrated, not segregated; and they are integrated in highly complex ways. Our daily experience of communication does not allow us to draw any sharp or constant distinction between them. The study of that integration and its complexity *is* the proper study of language: there is no other.

The integrationist therefore rejects the idea that verbal communication involves the kind of activity which allows the linguistic components to be distinguished from the non-linguistic and analysed systematically without reference to the latter. The integrationist's claim, on the contrary, is that any such segregation is impossible. Not just difficult or dubious in certain cases, but impossible in principle. It is the recognition of that impossibility which is the cornerstone of integrational linguistics.

The segregational approach has dominated the field of twentieth-century linguistics, particularly in the work of Saussure and his followers in Europe and of Bloomfield and his generativist successors in the USA. The integrational approach has been far less clearly articulated. Although there are significant strands of integrationist thinking in the linguistics of Sapir, Malinowski, Pike and Firth (Harris, 1998a), in none of these cases did this develop into anything more than a cautious modification of the prevailing segregationist programme. It always stopped short of calling in question whether the linguist is in a position to do what segregationists have claimed, on behalf of linguistics, to be able to do; namely, to identify by the application of objective criteria a determinate system of signs that constitutes 'the language' of a given community or a given individual. This challenge, which has been formulated increasingly explicitly in recent years, is at the core of current integrationist thinking.

Specific segregational assumptions and corresponding integrational counterproposals include the following.

(1) *Languages as systems.* The segregationist assumes the validity – and necessity – of drawing a sharp distinction between (i) languages as systems and (ii) the actual or possible use of these systems. This distinction is expressed in a variety of ways in segregational terminology (*langue* versus *parole*, 'competence' versus 'performance', 'code' versus 'message', etc.). The integrationist rejects any such distinction as simplistic and inadequate as a basis for understanding linguistic communication. The concept of 'a language', as far as the integrationist is concerned, is no more than a rather loosely defined generalization over a range of varied communicational practices. To what extent these practices are systematic is an open question and one to be addressed by reference to particular communication situations. But it is illusory to envisage a language from the start as a self-contained system of signs, equipped in advance to deal with all communication situations that could arise within a given community.

(2) *Communication and language use.* In accordance with (1), the segregationist assumes that, in order to engage in linguistic communication at all, it is necessary for the individual to have an appropriate system (i.e. a language) available for use. Consequently, the study of languages (systems) takes priority over the study of communication, which is merely one consequence of their use. The integrationist reverses this priority. That is to say, for the integrationist the study of communication comes first, because unless we can first analyse the relevant communicational process(es) we have no basis for constructing any rational account of what 'a language' is. In particular, it is only by studying linguistic communication that we can hope to discover what role, if any, the concept of 'a language' plays in people's communicational practices, what they regard the properties of a language as being, how or to what extent they distinguish between one language and another, and so on.

(3) *Languages as user-independent systems.* The segregationist assumes that languages are systems that exist in a stable form independently of their users: in other words, that the system does not change according to whoever happens to be using it. It is available, therefore, as 'the same system' for a potentially indefinite number of users. From this the segregationist proceeds to the further assumption that the system as such may legitimately be analysed at a level of generality which ignores the individual altogether. The integrationist, on the other hand, starts from the opposite assumption: that linguistics must never lose sight of the fact that communication always involves particular individuals acting in particular circumstances. There is no *a*

priori guarantee – nor could there be – which assures the linguist that particular individuals are merely implementing some user-independent system known in advance to all concerned. Whether or to what extent linguistic analysis needs any such assumption at all is, in the integrationist's view, debatable: it can never, in any case, simply be taken for granted.

(4) *Linguistic communities.* The segregationist assumes, in accordance with (3), that a linguistic community is a community whose members all use the same language. Thus, in effect, the community is defined by reference to the linguistic system, and not vice versa. This assumption is made quite explicit by those segregationists who postulate 'perfectly homogeneous' linguistic communities or 'ideal speaker-hearers'. (These two abstractions amount to the same thing for all theoretical purposes: they are the foundations of what might aptly be described as 'utopian' linguistics.) For the integrationist, on the other hand, a linguistic community is not a utopian fiction but an actual community whose members communicate verbally: there is no assumption that all use the same language(s), and no assumption about any level of linguistic proficiency that all share. This eliminates any need for inventing fabrications such as homogeneous communities or ideal speaker-hearers, which can lead only to the generation of bogus problems about language.

(5) *Languages as vocal systems.* Although it is not strictly required by any of (1-4) above, the segregationist typically assumes that languages are first and foremost *spoken* languages, i.e. systems of vocal signs. Mainstream linguistics throughout the twentieth century has been resolutely phonocentric. For the integrationist, this is a mistake in various respects. In the first place, because in face-to-face communication vocalization is only one component in an integrated series of activities which include gesture, gaze, facial expression, and bodily posture. (In fact, vocalization assumes the role of sole channel of linguistic communication only in a minority of situations, such as telephone conversations or talk between blind interlocutors.) Furthermore, writing is regarded by the segregationist as a secondary and derivative form of language, or else denied to be a form of language at all. Thus for the segregationist there is no essential difference between a preliterate linguistic community and a linguistic community of people who can read and write. For the integrationist, however, this difference is one of fundamental importance, since it affects the communicational practices of the community in countless details. In an integrational perspective, writing is no less a manifestation of language than speech. Furthermore, in the case of literate communities speech cannot be studied in isolation from writing, the two being integrated in a variety of ways.

(6) *Languages as rule systems.* The segregationist also tends to assume that languages are systems that exist or are 'represented' neurophysiologically in some way in the heads of their speakers. The system that members of any one linguistic community supposedly have in their heads is often said to be a system of rules. The rules in question are held to be – or to specify – complex pairings of sounds and meanings. Each such system determines what meaning, if any, is to be attached to any given sequence of sounds that speakers of that particular language might utter. Accordingly, the linguist's basic task is envisaged as being to find typical speakers of the language under investigation and to determine, as far as possible, what rules pair up the vocal forms of the language with their meanings, and what rules govern possible combinations both of forms and of meanings. The combinations admitted by the rules are claimed to be 'grammatical' and those prohibited 'ungrammatical'. To state these rules is regarded as providing a 'description' of the language. The integrationist, on the other hand, rejects both this concept of linguistic description and the concept of linguistic rules that goes with it, regarding both as based on confusions inherited from traditional European grammar. In particular, the integrationist dismisses as incoherent the notion that linguistic communication depends on following 'internalized' grammatical rules which we cannot make explicit and of which we are largely unaware (Baker and Hacker, 1984, pp.267-315).

The above points on which integrationists characteristically differ from segregationists might perhaps be summed up as follows. What is in contention as between the two approaches is whether, or to what extent, linguistics is entitled to decontextualize human linguistic behaviour in order to isolate, describe and explain various aspects of it. For the integrationist, all decontextualization distorts, and therefore the resultant linguistic descriptions and explanations, to the extent that they rely on decontextualized 'data', are automatically suspect. For they are no more than methodological artifacts of the oversimplifications from which they proceed. By presenting these artifacts as reliable accounts, on which further research may be based, the linguist succeeds only in diverting our attention from the actual conditions under which human beings have been able to develop their many and various language-making enterprises.

Theoretical compromises

One common reaction to the segregational/integrational opposition described above is to seek some compromise between the two approaches. It may be tempting to try to see the segregationist position as more persuasive on some points and the integrationist position as more persuasive on others. According to the integrationist, however, such compromises are themselves obfuscatory. It is not a question of choosing one's preferred combination of items from two alternative programmes on offer (as one might choose bacon-and-eggs off one breakfast menu, preceded or accompanied by muesli off an alternative vegetarian menu). Even less is there any question of pursuing both approaches simultaneously (pouring the dish of muesli over the bacon-and-eggs). For the features which distinguish the segregational approach from the integrational approach stand or fall together: they cannot be combined selectively to suit anyone's fancy. In short, these are diametrically opposed approaches to linguistic inquiry. Each gives ontological priority to a quite different order of 'facts'. And unless we see that this is so, and why it is so, we shall never think clearly about language. The choice is between taking 'the language system' as basic and explaining verbal communication in terms of its use; or taking communication as basic and explaining everything else in the linguistic domain by reference to the requirements this imposes on human behaviour. The beginning of wisdom in linguistics is to recognize this fundamental dichotomy. Only then shall we be in a position to distinguish between answering linguistic questions and begging them.

This should not be taken to mean that segregational analyses are of no interest at all from an integrational point of view. On the contrary, they often document and exemplify attitudes to linguistic issues which correspond in large measure to lay assumptions, particularly insofar as the latter have been moulded by Western cultural biases and pedagogic programmes. It is part of the integrationist project to examine how such assumptions about language arise and why they command widespread – even blind – acceptance. But this cannot be done unless orthodox linguistics is itself subject to critical scrutiny and its basic premises questioned, rather than being accepted as transcendental wisdom. Nor does the integrationist wish to deny that, for certain purposes and in certain circumstances, segregational notions may be useful. The bone of contention, rather, concerns the validity of the way these notions 'operate as the foundations of contemporary theorizing about language and communication' (Toolan, 1996, p.10).

The development of modern linguistics shows that the segregational approach has been publicly and predominantly assumed to be 'right', or even the only possible approach. Segregationism has been the orthodox doctrine which underpins the establishment of linguistics as a study entitled to its own place in the modern university curriculum. The academic acceptance of segregational assumptions has had much to do with sustained efforts to obtain for linguistics institutional recognition as an independent discipline. And this in turn is connected with the professional status that linguists have sought for themselves and with their claims to be acknowledged as society's 'experts' on linguistic matters. Here too the integrationist takes a quite different view.

Linguistics and the linguist

In orthodox textbooks, the linguist is implicitly cast from the beginning in an especially privileged role. The privileges include (i) a wealth of insight into what language is and how its affairs are conducted (even when, in the same breath, it is announced that these are *goals* of linguistic inquiry); (ii) the ability to determine in advance the boundaries of any given linguistic phenomenon and the appropriate methods to be employed in its investigation; (iii) a grandstand view of the linguistic history of the world, based on the work of previous generations of linguists; and (iv) the right to be recognized as an authority *qua* 'scientist' in the field of language. All these privileges are presumptions of linguistic authority which the integrationist rejects.

The claim to authority most popular among segregationists is the claim that (their) linguistics is a 'science'. Thus *qua* linguists they speak as 'scientists'. As linguistic 'scientists' they expect to enjoy a prestige which will elevate them to parity of esteem with physicists, chemists, biologists and other practitioners of the natural sciences. This kind of claim was first put forward on behalf of linguistics in the nineteenth century (Müller, 1864, p.1; Harris, 1992). It has often been accepted at face value by the general public, largely because (i) the laity stands in awe of clever people who can speak, or speak about, a number of different languages, and (ii) academic linguistics has invented an impressive technical jargon of its own which is just as impenetrable to the lay person as the jargon of doctors, electrical engineers and other specialists. Thus it readily appears that the linguist has all the trappings of professional expertise.

For instance, it has become the hallmark of the modern professional linguist to talk not about sounds but about 'phonemes' and 'allophones'; not about words but about 'morphemes' and 'lexemes'; not about saying something but about 'illocutionary acts'; and so on. The more obscure the jargon, the better. At least, for those linguists who like to pose as scientists. But the fact is that, unlike their colleagues in the natural sciences, academic linguists find it difficult to agree among themselves about how to define their own basic technical terms. (Some two hundred different definitions of the 'sentence' have been proposed.) Nor can they agree on what practical procedures to adopt in linguistic investigations, or reach a consensus about what constitutes a 'linguistic fact'. This is a sorry state of affairs, but it is one which the integrationist faces up to and addresses, recognizing that one cannot convert traditional school grammar into a 'science' by dressing up its distinctions in a new garb.

Nor can it be said that linguistics shares with physics, chemistry, etc. the application of 'the experimental method', which requires that results must be strictly 'replicable'. It does not take much reflection to realize that linguistics does not fit happily into any such tradition of inquiry. What kind of experiment would determine how many parts of speech there are in *Thank you very much, madam* ? Or how many words? Such questions have nothing in common with determining the composition of water or the structure of cells.

Linguistics as hocus-pocus

Integrationists' scepticism about the scientific status of linguistics is sometimes taken as allegiance to the **'hocus-pocus'** approach to language studies. This term alludes to a debate that arose between partisans of two conflicting views of linguistic description, and is explained as follows in a current dictionary of linguistics:

> A phrase coined in the 1950s to characterise one of two extreme states of mind in a hypothetical linguist who sets up a description of linguistic data; opposed to God's truth. 'Hocus-pocus' linguists approach data in the expectation that they will have to impose an organisation on it in order to show structural patterns. Different linguists, on this view, could approach the same data, and by virtue of their different backgrounds, intuitions, procedures, etc., arrive at differing descriptions. In a 'God's truth' approach, by contrast, the aim is to demonstrate an underlying structure really present in the data over which there could be no dispute. (Crystal, 1991, p.166)

The reference in this account to 'a hypothetical linguist' perhaps gives the misleading impression that the difference between a 'hocus-pocus' approach and a 'God's-truth' approach was only ever a matter of idle speculation. This was far from being the case, since it bore directly not only on the status of linguistics as a 'science' but also on issues of methodology. The question of what kind of truth a 'God's-truth' linguist claimed for linguistic description was another matter. One answer was that linguistic description should describe **'psychological reality'**, a view associated in particular with the work of Saussure. Saussure construed this requirement as meaning that the units, distinctions and categories set up by the linguist should correspond to those that speakers of 'the language' actually deployed, consciously or unconsciously, in speaking it. Thus, for example, the question of how many distinct English words there are with the form *cat* ([kat]) would be a 'psychologically real' question, and not one to be settled by some classificatory decision imposed by the linguist (whether arbitrary or not). In contrast to this, there were other linguists (successors, not contemporaries, of Saussure's) who explicitly disavowed the idea that there was any 'fact' of the matter to report; or that, even if there were, it should necessarily bind the linguist in deciding to opt for one classification rather than another. Accordingly, different descriptions might well recognize a different number of English 'words' in the same corpus of 'data': a state of affairs not conducive to convincing anyone of the objectivity of the 'linguistic' approach. For what is at issue here would patently be disagreement between linguists over how to define and identify what seems to be an important unit in verbal communication, i.e. 'the word' (Davis, H.G., 1997).

Saussure's insistence on 'psychological reality' (although he did not himself use that expression) in linguistic descriptions related to his epistemological stance. In order to establish the credentials of linguistics as a 'science', it was essential for a theorist of Saussure's generation to identify something to which the linguist's descriptions were accountable. For this was the hallmark of a science. The physicist, the botanist, the geologist, etc. were all engaged in the production of descriptions which took some aspect of reality as their describienda and could be tested for accuracy. A non-descriptive science was a contradiction in terms. That was why disciplines which relied more on argument, assumption and opinion than on observation – disciplines such as philosophy and literature – were not generally regarded as 'sciences'. Saussure was very clear about where he wanted linguistics to belong: not with philosophy and literature but with the sciences.

The 'hocus-pocus' position presented a challenge to this epistemological stance, precisely because it treated linguistic description as a matter of imposing order on the available evidence rather than a matter of discovering and reporting an order that was already there. Consequently, linguistic description was to be judged ultimately by its own internal consistency rather than on its correspondence point-by-point to each piece of observable 'data'. A parallel but more general epistemological debate in philosophy centred on the notion of 'truth': was it 'correspondence' to an independent reality (Russell, 1912) or 'internal coherence' of some conceptual scheme (Joachim, 1906)?

The hocus-pocus approach would have been totally unacceptable to Saussure, who insists time and again that linguistic facts are realities and not abstractions conjured up by the linguist. Paradoxically, however, (at least, according to some critics) Saussure was instrumental in setting up a rather rigid theoretical framework into which the linguist's observations had to be fitted.

Some theorists tried to resolve this conflict by having the best of both worlds. Thus we find both the 'hocus-pocus' and the 'God's-truth' position sometimes distinguished from a third position where it is assumed that

> the linguist's abstractions are also abstracted, albeit unconsciously, by native speakers of the language as the product of certain innate mental structures and as the result of their having learned the language in childhood, and are part of the content of the speakers' minds or brains. (Robins, 1989, p.44)

There is no generally accepted term for this third position, but it seems apt to call it 'holy-pocus', since without the intervention of some supernatural agency it is difficult to see how there could be any assurance that all speakers unconsciously perform exactly the same analyses as the linguist consciously performs.

Where does the integrationist stand in all this? The question ultimately comes down to what a 'linguistic fact' is − if there indeed is such a thing − and, if there is, how a linguist can recognize it. This will be discussed in more detail later (see Ch.3, Ch.4, Ch.6). For the moment it suffices to say that the integrationist is not a 'God's-truth' linguist, nor a 'hocus-pocus' linguist, nor yet a 'holy-pocus' linguist. What the integrationist will point out is that one of the fatal mistakes made by the architects of orthodox linguistics was to have set up in anticipation a supposed domain of 'linguistic facts' for scientific description, but to have wed this proposal to specific doctrines about language and languages which were bound to thwart any plausible identification of the facts in question. It is a curious case of a discipline committed in advance to self-inflicted injury. What the integrationist claims is not that there are no linguistic facts, but that orthodox linguistics looks for them in the wrong place.

The conditions of linguistic inquiry

Integrational linguistics rejects any spurious claims-in-advance to scientific validity, of the kind that have become rhetorical commonplaces in introductory textbooks on linguistics. The integrationist leaves open any judgment on the status of the linguist's conclusions or methods and starts with a critical examination of the conditions which make linguistic inquiry possible. In so doing, inevitably, the integrationist questions the linguist's credentials. This is the essential first step, which orthodox linguistics invariably omits, doubtless because raising that question is already a professional embarrassment for self-proclaimed 'scientists'. The integrationist insists on including it for very fundamental reasons, which are: 1. *Linguistics itself presupposes the validity of certain forms of communication, and the pronouncements of the linguist cannot escape judgment as a communicational enterprise. 2. The linguist in the end has no other basis of expertise than that available to any lay member of the community; namely the linguistic experience acquired by participation in the processes of communication.*

When these two reasons are given their full due, it becomes apparent that integrationists are not merely proposing a few minor reforms or modifications to the orthodox programme for linguistics, but insisting on a radical overhaul of its theoretical basis. To the segregationist, this will doubtless appear as subversion. So be it. Linguists are not people who have done more communicating than anyone else, or are conspicuously better at it (they are often conspicuously bad at it), or have thought about it more deeply, or brought superior intellectual powers to bear on their own linguistic observations. Any of these might be possible reasons for deference to the professional linguist, but none of them stands up to serious examination.

That is why linguistic inquiry, if it is not to beg important questions, must begin by examining its own *modus operandi*. It is in this sense that, for the integrationist, linguistics has to be seen as 'constituting its own subject matter' (Love, 1998). There can be no *a priori* assumption that the linguist already knows better than anyone else what to look for in language, where to look for it, and how. But that is what has been assumed by the theorists of linguistic orthodoxy for most of the twentieth century.

Mainstream linguistics, in short, has a rather narrow, built-in cultural bias. Having its roots in Western traditional grammar, it assumes that the proper or natural basis for being a linguist is the kind of education afforded by membership of a European nation (or one of its colonies or former colonies). This means, in effect, membership of a literate society in which literacy has a common alphabetic basis. The irony of this situation is that no such basis has ever been available to the great majority of the world's linguistic communities.

If contemporary linguistics is to be rescued from this ethnocentric myopia (as an integrationist would hope) it must find a perspective from which 'expertise' in linguistic matters is not equated with the self-serving professionalism that marked the rise of the subject to academic independence in Western universities during the nineteenth and twentieth centuries. The erection of academic barriers between linguistics and other subjects can lead only to a narrower, more blinkered view of language. The integrationist is therefore wary of the notion that linguistics is best left to 'linguists'.

This caveat about expertise can be put in a more positive way. Language belongs to the whole human race. It follows, as far as the integrationist is concerned, that **everybody is a linguist**. And necessarily so. Whether we are 'educated' or not: whether we are 'literate' or not. For all human beings engage in analytic reflection about their own linguistic experience: this is a *sine qua non* of engaging in language itself. Unless human beings were capable of this analytic reflection, then questions such as 'What is your name?', 'What is this called?' and 'What does this mean?' could never be asked, let alone answered. But recognizing everybody as a linguist does not mean that everybody is right about language, any more than recognizing everybody as a member of society means than everybody is right about society.

The sender-receiver model of communication

When we consider it exclusively from the point of view of the individuals involved, communication always appears to be a voluntary activity undertaken *in addition to* other activities. Speech is something 'extra', something more than just remaining silent: it requires making an effort. So does listening. Communication between individuals demands at the minimum engaging the attention of – or paying attention to – at least one other person.

Theorists of communication have seldom failed to recognize this elementary fact. Unfortunately, they have often failed to get much further. The result is a severely restricted view of communication, frequently adopted by segregationists. It is known as the 'sender – receiver' model of communication.

This model represents communication as a transaction between two hypothetical individuals, *A* and *B*. *A* is the 'sender' and *B* the 'receiver'. *A* is supposed to have a message and wishes to send that message to *B*. In order to send the message, *A* has to 'encode' it in a particular form, and then transmit it via a certain medium to *B*. who receives it and then 'decodes' it.

So the model has a very limited number of components that need to be taken into account: in fact, just seven. These are:

(i) the sender
(ii) the receiver
(iii) the message
(iv) the code
(v) the encoding process
(vi) the transmission
(vii) the decoding process.

These seven are in practice reduced to six if the decoding process is taken to be a simple reversal of the encoding process.

The classic application of this model to language is to be found in the work of Saussure, who drafted what became the Magna Carta of orthodox modern linguistics: his *Cours de linguistique générale.* What Saussure called the 'speech circuit' is envisaged as operating as follows.

> The starting point of the circuit is in the brain of one individual, for instance *A*, where facts of consciousness which we shall call concepts are associated with representations of linguistic signs or sound patterns by means of which they may be expressed. Let us suppose that a given concept triggers in the brain a corresponding sound pattern. This is an entirely *psychological* phenomenon, followed in turn by a *physiological* process: the brain transmits to the organs of phonation an impulse corresponding to the pattern. Then sound waves are sent from *A*'s mouth to *B*'s ear: a purely *physical* process. Next, the circuit continues in *B* in the opposite order: from ear to brain, the physiological transmission of the sound pattern; in the brain, the psychological association of this pattern with the corresponding concept. If *B* speaks in turn, this new act will pursue - from his brain to *A*'s - exactly the same course as the first, passing through the same successive phases... (Saussure, 1922, p.28).

This we may call for convenience the 'talking heads' model of speech communication. It is illustrated in Saussure's book by a diagram showing two heads, those of *A* and *B*, linked by lines going from *A*'s brain, via *A*'s mouth, to *B*'s ear, and thence to *B*'s brain, and from *B*'s brain, via *B*'s mouth, to *A*'s ear and thence to *A*'s brain.

Since its introduction by Saussure, the 'talking heads' model has been the mainstay of segregational linguistics. (For more recent statements of the model see, for instance, Katz, 1966, pp.103f.; Chafe, 1970, p.17; Moulton, 1970, pp.23ff.; Crystal, 1980, pp.54ff.; Matthei and Roeper, 1983, pp.13ff. Some of these subdivide the speech circuit into more than the seven components identified above, but the essentials remain unchanged.)

At first sight it might seem that the 'talking heads' model is perfectly compatible with an integrational approach to communication. Does it not represent the whole process as an integration of various distinct activities by the speaker and the hearer? Does it not explain this integration as linked via the concepts common to the initiation of encoding and the termination of decoding? Does it not locate those points of integration quite precisely in the sequence of activities? And does it not identify the integrational instrument as 'the language' which *A* and *B* both know?

This language, Saussure's *Cours* tells us quite specifically, 'can be localised in that particular section of the speech circuit where sound patterns are associated with concepts' (Saussure, 1922, p.31). In other words, it is a 'psychologically real' system existing in certain places in the brain of *A* and the brain of *B*, where the associations between sounds and concepts are stored.

On first inspection of the model, it may be difficult to see what more an integrationist could possibly want.

If so, the appearance is deceptive. Saussure's model is segregationist through and through. To see this, we have to realize that the model has certain implications that are not immediately apparent in Saussure's initial presentation of it. The most important are as follows.

1. The model implies that communication is **'telementational'**, i.e. that communication is a process of thought-transference from one person's mind to another's.

2. The model implies that communication is successful only if the concept that originally triggered the start of the process in A's brain is the same as the concept that is eventually triggered in B's brain. (Otherwise it would not matter what happened in B's brain, provided a concept of some kind was triggered.)

3. This matching requirement in turn implies that for successful communication a **fixed code** must be in operation. This code, in the case of speech, is A's and B's common language (*la langue* in Saussurean terminology). If each were using a different code, i.e. speaking a different language from the other, then again communication would break down.

4. This in turn implies that the code itself provides the relevant pairings of sounds and concepts. In other words, the linguistic sign is already taken to be a unit which associates a specific sound pattern and a specific concept in the mind – this association, and nothing else, being *itself constitutive of the sign*. That this is the correct interpretation of Saussure's model there is no doubt: Saussure himself spells it out at some length. Each linguistic sign unites a sound pattern (*signifiant*) and a concept (*signifié*). Thus the sign is assumed to be determinate with respect to both form and meaning.

All four of these implications associated with the 'talking heads' model have to be rejected if linguistic inquiry is to be conducted in accordance with integrationist principles.

The missing context

No less important in the integrationist critique of the 'talking heads' model of communication is drawing attention to what the model omits altogether. What is missing includes the following.

We do not know who these people A and B are, where they come from, or what the relationship between them is. We do not know where they are, or who else is present. We do not know what sounds they are uttering or what they are talking about. The illustration in Saussure's text appears to show them in a face-to-face situation, where presumably they would be able to make eye contact and observe each other's facial expressions and movements (unless one or both were blind – but this we do not know either). In other words, the whole episode which is supposedly typical of speech communication is totally decontextualized. And because of the decontextualization we have no means of judging how what is said is integrated with whatever is *not* said but is nevertheless communicationally relevant. Speech becomes a quite pointless activity if this integration cannot be effected.

For an integrationist, this means that the model is not only useless but totally misleading. By decontextualizing the speech act in which *A* and *B* are engaged, it misrepresents the basic conditions under which communication takes place. It is like a model which describes travel as a process of moving from one place to another, but at such a level of abstraction that we do not know who is travelling, where to or where from, and what form of transport is being used.

The integrationist objection to sender-receiver models is that there simply are no forms of communication of this kind: that is, there is no such thing as a decontextualized communication process, any more than there is a decontextualized form of travel. As soon as an attempt is made to remedy this deficit by building in specific information about speakers, topics and circumstances, the model straight away loses its generality. Just as, once we specify that transport is by air, the travel model ceases to be of very much use for cyclists.

The first thing an integrationist will insist on in linguistics is that any viable model of linguistic communication must treat *all* the activities concerned – not just some of them – as integrated activities. This means that communication *must be contextualized*. Context is not an optional extra. It is not just a backdrop that can be changed at will, as in a theatrical performance. (For further discussion of the notion 'context', see Ch.4.)

Linguistic 'observation'

Examining the 'talking heads' model in more depth will make it clear why integrationists insist on the importance of elucidating the conditions of linguistic inquiry itself.

The 'talking heads' model tacitly places the linguist in the position of a neutral third-party observer. This observer simply 'takes in', *qua* intelligent bystander, the exchange between *A* and *B*. Having taken it in, the observant linguist-bystander will proceed to analyse it, and so become an investigator. The investigator will thus have available 'at first hand' the public evidence of what can be seen and heard; but this will not include, patently, observation of what is going on either inside the head of *A* or inside the head of *B*. Thus the investigator's account of what *A* is saying to *B* or *B* to *A* will be based on interpretation from a perspective which cannot take into account some of the information directly known to *A* and *B*; namely, information about their own thoughts, feelings, intentions, etc. Immediately and inevitably, the question arises whether the investigator's interpretation of the speech act coincides with the interpretations of the participants themselves. There are relations between at least three presumably relevant interpretations to be considered: *A*'s interpretation, *B*'s interpretation, and the investigator's.

Now a plausible lay assumption would be the following: that if any credence at all is to be attached to the third of these interpretations, the investigator must already be familiar with 'the language' that *A* and *B* are speaking. (Otherwise it is difficult to see what are the investigator's credentials for conducting the investigation in the first place.) Which in turn assumes not only (i) many prior similarities in patterns of linguistic experience as between *A*, *B* and the investigator, but also (ii) that the investigator is able reliably to integrate relevant aspects of certain prior linguistic experiences with the current linguistic experience, i.e. of the linguistic exchange between *A* and *B* now under observation. Thus, for instance, if *A* and *B* are speaking English, the assumption has to be that the investigator is no less communicationally proficient in English than *A* and *B* are. More generally, *whatever* language *A* and *B* are speaking the linguist has to be at least as well acquainted with it as they are. But where does this assurance come from?

Once we raise this question, it becomes clear that the 'talking heads' model of communication incorporates a concealed circularity. It tacitly assumes that *there is* a language (call it *L*), such that *A*, *B* and the investigator are severally proficient at communication-in-*L*, and are so *independently of the current episode of communication or any arbitrarily selected episode.*

The point is important. And the point is not just that, according to this model, languages can be (reliably) investigated only by those already communicationally proficient in them. The more general issue is that this conclusion, *pace* Saussure, makes it impossible to treat languages as 'objects' available for neutral inspection by the professional linguist. The parallel with the professional astronomer observing the stars, or the professional botanist observing plants, breaks down. For the linguist, unlike the astronomer or the botanist, already has a vested interest; namely, an interest in showing that the investigator is no less knowledgeable than those whose behaviour is under investigation. Should it turn out otherwise, then the competence of the linguist is automatically called in question. And once this happens, the credibility of the model begins to collapse.

Adopting such a model, in short, ties the hands of the linguist in advance. It does so by *presupposing* that *A*, *B* and the linguist are all equally proficient in the language *L* under investigation. As far as the integrationist is concerned, that is simply not acceptable as a condition – or rather precondition – of linguistic inquiry. It begs all kinds of questions about what linguistic proficiency consists in and how it should be measured. Wherever linguistic inquiry starts, it cannot – for the integrationist – start there.

Where *does* it start, then? In order to answer this question, let us probe the validity of the 'talking heads' model a little further.

Linguistic reflexivity

Let us imagine that *A* and *B*, instead of talking to each other, are playing tennis. Our model, in other words, is no longer a model of speech communication, but a model of the game taking place on court, with *A* and *B* as the players. The transmission lines linking the two protagonists will no longer go from mouth to ear, but from racquet to racquet, following the trajectory of the ball. Nevertheless, it is still a form of interaction between *A*'s behaviour and *B*'s behaviour that is being modelled. In this analogy, the role of the descriptive linguist will be matched (roughly) by that of a tennis commentator viewing the match from the spectators' stand.

In both cases, the requirements of description and commentary impose certain desiderata on whoever plays the role of third-party observer. In the case of tennis, clearly, the first requirement for being a good commentator is a thorough knowledge of how to play tennis; for without that knowledge no one could make much sense of what the players were doing, let alone describe it intelligently. As in the linguistic case, the commentator would need to have this knowledge *in advance* of describing the play in progress: no one supposes that the relevant information could be acquired simply by inspection of the events as they unfolded. So again, a serious account of what is going on presupposes *the observer's* ability to integrate present experience with past experience: a competent Wimbledon commentator cannot be someone who has never seen a tennis ball or a tennis racquet before.

The great difference between tennis commentary and linguistic commentary is this. Tennis commentary does not require the commentator to play tennis; whereas, *mutatis mutandis*, that is exactly the requirement imposed on the linguistic commentator. In other words, linguistic description of the verbal activity of *A* and *B* requires *the linguist also* to engage in verbal activity. Linguistics itself is a linguistic exercise; whereas tennis commentary is not a form of tennis.

In order to describe or discuss the linguistic activities of others, we must ourselves engage in linguistic activity of our own. What makes this both possible and necessary? This is the question that takes us to the heart of linguistic inquiry. And the integrationist answer is that language (unlike tennis) is **reflexive**. It is only through the reflexivity of language that linguistics is possible.

What this means is that language itself has to provide the means by which linguistic phenomena may be analysed and linguistic information given. We cannot get 'outside' language in order to do this: on the contrary, we have no option but to remain 'within' the confines of language if our attempts at linguistic analysis are to be successful. We must be able to ask questions about language and propose answers to those questions. But questions and answers *are themselves linguistic operations*.

If you now ask (seriously) 'But what is a question?' or 'What is an answer?', the best reply anyone can give you is that a question is the kind of thing you are now asking and an answer is what you are now being given. Explanation stops there. You may not like that response, of course. You may perhaps object that all it does is turn the questions back upon the questioner. Just so. It exploits the reflexivity of language to deal with a problem that arises out of that reflexivity. And that is all that language allows us to do. If you have not yet grasped that, then you have understood very little about linguistic questions or possible linguistic answers. We cannot at will step outside language in order to demonstrate to sceptics how it works. Any more than someone can step off the top floor of the Empire State Building in order to demonstrate how gravity operates, hoping all the while that the demonstration itself will somehow be exempt from the law it exemplifies. If the world worked like that, presumably we should be inundated with demonstrators quite unworried about the consequences of hitting the ground below.

According to the integrationist, it is the reflexivity of language which makes linguistics fundamentally different from all other forms of inquiry into human affairs. And linguistic inquiry begins with the questions we all ask about language as part of own linguistic apprenticeship. Some of these questions have already been mentioned above ('What is your name?', 'What is this called?', 'What does this word mean?'), but there are many more. These are **metalinguistic** questions and the terms in which they are formulated are metalinguistic terms ('name', 'word', 'mean', 'question', 'answer', etc.). It is the provision of metalinguistic terminology which is both the hallmark of linguistic reflexivity and the facilitating mechanism for linguistic inquiry. Asking even the simplest questions about what A is saying to B, and how linguists are in a position to interpret and describe this, takes us immediately into the metalinguistic domain. It is reflexivity which makes it possible to compile dictionaries and write grammars, both of which are exercises in metalinguistics.

Thus, according to the integrationist, any sense we can make of language has to be made *within* the resources of language. The question 'What is a question?' can be asked only by those already familiar with the reflexive dimension of language. And any answer is similarly constrained. Such constraints govern all our analytic reflections on language. The point is so basic that it is easily overlooked. *Linguistic inquiry is conditional on the reflexivity of language.* This is what gives us the possibility of asking and answering metalinguistic questions.

The 'talking heads' model effaces linguistic reflexivity by simply ignoring it. It is a model which assumes that in some culture-neutral sense it is perfectly clear what is going on both (i) when anonymous A speaks to anonymous B, and also (ii) when an anonymous linguist proposes some account of what A and B are saying. And this is one basic respect in which the model is segregationist: it presupposes that linguistic inquiry – and linguistic theory in general – can somehow be divorced from a consideration of the particular circumstances in which it arises and the conditions of linguistic reflexivity which make it possible. For the integrationist this is an unacceptable premise.

Once sufficient attention is paid to these foundational conditions, we soon see that they have many ramifications. They undermine positions which the majority of twentieth-century linguists have always taken for granted. That is the price a discipline has to pay for not beginning at the beginning.

Reflexive and non-reflexive communication

To eliminate one possible confusion straight away, it may be worth remarking that reflexive communication has nothing to do with talking to yourself. You could talk to yourself, if you felt so inclined, even if language were non-reflexive. But it isn't.

Reflexivity is not a property common to *all* forms of communication. Many familiar communication systems *do not have it*. If you want to study language, this is the first thing you have to realize. Language is a form of communication: but it is, in this respect, quite different from certain other forms of communication with which we are familiar.

Take traffic lights, for instance. Red, amber and green signals play a contrastive communicational role which motorists and other road-users recognize. But the system of lights does not include any 'metasignals' which mean 'red', 'amber' or 'green'. This is hardly surprising, since directing traffic at intersections is a very restricted communicational function and it is difficult to see what purpose such sophistications would serve. Similarly, sounding your horn to warn an oblivious pedestrian of your approach is a useful communicational device for motorists to have available. But it does not need to be backed up by metasignals meaning 'I am about to sound my horn' or 'I have just sounded my horn'. In these simple cases the absence of reflexivity is readily understandable.

More puzzling, perhaps, is that we find very rich and highly developed forms of communication which lack reflexivity. Pictorial communication, for example, is in general non-reflexive. This is often misunderstood by people who point out that it is possible to draw a picture of a picture: so it is, but that is not the criterion of reflexivity. Reflexivity is not a matter of mere replication or reproduction. Nor is it a matter of self-reference. Taking a photograph of yourself taking a photograph of yourself in the mirror does not produce a reflexive image on the film in your camera.

Pictorial communication is non-reflexive because and insofar as it incorporates no pictorial metasigns, i.e. has no subset of pictorial forms, devices or techniques dedicated solely to the depiction of pictures. We do not find this in any of the world's great pictorial traditions. (Whereas all the great linguistic traditions – and minor traditions too – have a developed metalinguistic terminology of some kind, although it is often very different from that which provides the foundation for Western language studies. Cf. Stross, 1974; Calame-Griaule, 1987.)

How about the use of scale models in architecture and engineering? Is not this a spatial metalanguage, in which small objects 'stand for' larger ones in a systematic way? Can we not sometimes solve problems of construction by simulating them in miniature rather than tackling them directly at the full scale level? Yes, we can. But none of this gives us an exact analogue to linguistic reflexivity. For even if no one had ever thought of building scale models, nevertheless erecting buildings would still be possible. The point about verbal metalanguage is that without it language as we know it would *not* be possible.

Try to imagine English shorn of all its metalinguistic equipment. At first sight it might seem as though little has changed. We should apparently still be able to say 'Hello!', 'Goodbye!', 'The cat sat on the mat', and many other things. We could even get by without dictionaries and grammars, as many civilizations in the past have done. But we are overlooking something much more fundamental. In non-reflexive English, it would be impossible to ask anyone to repeat what they had just said, let alone ask them what it meant. We have to realize that 'repetition' and 'meaning' are metalinguistic concepts, every bit as much as 'name' or 'word' or 'sentence'. And unless such notions were available to us, we should have to be able to make sense of our own linguistic experience in a very different way from that to which we are accustomed. It is even arguable that, shorn of reflexivity, we should be unable to make much sense of language at all. Perhaps that is why your dog answers to the call 'Rover!' (and so manifests his grasp of one elementary communicational game) but still does not understand that *Rover* is his name, and even less that many other dogs might have the same name as he.

The professional linguist's jargon of 'phonemes', 'morphemes', 'lexemes' and all the rest is simply an extension of lay metalanguage. It has no other basis. That is why there is no need to stand in awe of it, and why it must, if it is to make sense at all, reduce to concepts already implicit in our lay vocabulary. In this respect, it is very *unlike* the current terminology of physics, chemistry and the natural sciences: for this latter terminology does *not* reduce to notions already implicit in our everyday ways of talking about the world of nature.

Communication as integration

The sender-receiver model, in all its various versions, proposes a chain of events in which communication is defined by what happens at either end of the chain. The initial and the terminal states of the process have to match or correspond in some way (*B*'s concept with *A*'s concept, *B*'s understanding with *A*'s intention, the 'message' received with the 'message' sent). What happens in between is merely incidental, and of interest only insofar as it speeds 'the message' on its way without loss or interference.

To this integrationism opposes a quite different concept of communication, in which it is the process itself, and not what happens at either end, that matters. And it matters because managing the process is a matter of survival. It requires those engaged in it to integrate their activities over time in such a way that the continuity of the process itself is preserved and rationalized. This concept embraces much that the sender-receiver model excludes in its attempt to reduce communication to an *interaction* between *A* and *B*. The integrationist view allows into consideration all the *non-interactive* forms of behaviour that play such a vital role in sustaining integration, including those forms of self-communication that we often call 'thinking'. It is one of the blatant ironies of the sender-receiver model that although telementation plays a key role in defining the criteria for initial and terminal states of the communication process, nevertheless thinking is systematically excluded from the process itself. It can occur 'before' and 'after' but not 'during' (i.e. as part of) communication.

For the integrationist, therefore, communication is not an optional extra to some more basic programme. There is no 'more basic programme' in human existence. In other words, this integration of activities is something we have to take part in, whether we like it or not. It is a necessary condition of life as we know it. We are born into a world that requires us to communicate, to integrate one kind of activity with another and with the corresponding activities of other people. If we manage the integrational task successfully, we live. If not, we die.

The same overriding necessity for integration applies to every individual as well as to every society. A society in which communication starts to break down is a society whose days are numbered. A society in which communication has become impossible is a society already dead: it has *dis*-integrated. A relationship between two people for whom communication has broken down is likewise in a state of *dis*-integration. A person who can no longer integrate today's experiences with yesterday's, or plan for tomorrow, is a person for whom even self-communication has broken down; and any such *dis*-integration of the self destroys the only basis on which language is possible.

For the integrationist, the possibilities and the limits of human communication, both in general and in any given instance, are governed by three kinds of factor:

(i) **biomechanical**

(ii) **macrosocial**

(iii) **circumstantial**.

Biomechanical factors relate to the physical and mental capacities of the human being. *Macrosocial* factors relate to practices established in the community or some group within the community. *Circumstantial* factors relate to the specifics of particular situations. Thus the fact that A and B communicate in speech only via sounds of a certain amplitude and frequency is a biomechanical factor, having to do with the physiological constitution of the human body. The fact that A and B cannot communicate in Swahili because B knows no Swahili (even though A does) is a macrosocial factor. The fact that A can speak to B even though separated by a distance of thousands of miles (because a telephone is available) is a circumstantial factor.

It is possible to consider biomechanical, macrosocial and circumstantial factors independently of one another. But any episode of communication will involve the integration of all three. That is to say, communication in any form will impose on the participants requirements of a biomechanical, macrosocial and circumstantial nature and to organize their participation in such a way that these requirements do not conflict.

Language as a mode of communication is no more exempt from these requirements than any other mode of communication. But linguistic communication has certain properties which are not shared by all modes of communication, and one of these properties, reflexivity, is crucial to understanding both the possibilities and the limitations of linguistic inquiry. It is by drawing attention to these possibilities and limitations that integrational linguistics aims to change the way people think about language. In so doing, it seeks an emancipation from the restrictions imposed by a view of human communication that has long been dominant in Western culture.

Further reading

- Harris and Wolf, 1998, Part 1, 'Language and Communication'
- On metalanguage: Stross, 1974; Davis, H.G., 1997
- On linguistic 'rules': Baker and Hacker, 1984, Ch.8
- On Saussure: Harris, 1987b
- On self-communication: Harris, 1996c, Ch.11

Questions for discussion

1. 'If we observed closely enough, we should find that no two persons – or rather, perhaps, no one person at different times – spoke exactly alike.' (L. Bloomfield) If this is true, what problems does it raise for segregational linguistics?

2. 'Linguistic theory is concerned primarily with an ideal speaker-listener, in a completely homogeneous speech-community.' (N. Chomsky) Why would an integrationist object to this claim?

3. 'The very essence of language is the correlation between sound on the one hand and meaning on the other.' (W.G. Moulton) Is this a position that an integrationist would accept?

4. '*Elephant* is a noun in English.' What questions would an integrationist want to put to a linguist who made this statement?

5. 'The most important claim linguists make is that their study of language is scientific.' (F.P. Dinneen) Why would an integrationist challenge that claim?

6. What are the (i) biomechanical, (ii) macrosocial and (iii) circumstantial conditions that you had to fulfil in order to read this page?

2

Language and the Language Myth

Languages are often regarded as occupying an intermediate position between language (as a human 'faculty') and speech (as a human activity). It may therefore at first sight appear paradoxical that there are linguists who are seriously prepared to question whether languages exist. (Doesn't everyone know that English is a different language from French?) For if these sceptics are right, then it would follow that most of modern linguistics, not to mention more traditional forms of language-teaching, would have been based upon no more than a myth.

The history of the language myth

What integrationists call 'the language myth' has a long history in the West. In its modern form it is a cultural product of post-Renaissance Europe and the rigid political divisions into autonomous nation-states that are a feature of that period of European history. 'One country – one language' was the ideal to which all the major centralising monarchies aspired. Compiling dictionaries and grammars of one's mother tongue became a patriotic enterprise. In certain instances academies were established, sometimes under royal patronage, in order to give authoritative rulings on linguistic matters, so that there should be no doubt about what the proper form of the national language was. Under such regimes it became increasingly difficult to defend publicly the linguistic rights of minorities or to treat linguistic non-conformity of any kind as other than a deviation from an officially sanctioned norm. In this sense, the language myth was a political myth, designed to serve the ends of nationalism. Educational systems were set up with the express design of converting that myth into a nation-wide reality.

The theory underlying the language myth, however, had much deeper roots in European culture. It was based on two ancient theses about communication. Although these two theses are logically independent, they lend each other powerful support. One is the thesis that speech is a form of **telementation**, a means of conveying thoughts from one mind to another. The other thesis is that of linguistic determinacy: it holds that every effective form of communication requires a **fixed code**.

The telementation thesis and the determinacy thesis are independent of each other in the sense that even if we agree that speech is a matter of conveying thoughts from one person's mind to another's, it does not follow that this has to be done by adopting a fixed code. Likewise, even if we agree that all effective communication requires the use of a fixed code, we do not have to concede that speech is telementational. (Behaviourists, for example, have often explicitly rejected the mentalism implied in the most common formulations of the telementation thesis: Bloomfield, 1935, pp.142ff.) However, it is certainly convenient – to say the least – if the two theses are taken in tandem, because telementation provides an explanation of how fixed codes function and what they are for, while fixed codes in turn provide an explanation, in principle, of how telementation is possible. In fact, in the history of Western thought there turns out to be a close connexion between the two: they almost always go together.

This connexion can be clearly seen in the version of the language myth given by the English philosopher John Locke:

> Man, though he have great variety of thoughts, and such from which others as well as himself might receive profit and delight; yet they are all within his own breast, invisible and hidden from others, nor can of themselves be made to appear. The comfort and advantage of society not being to be had without communication of thoughts, it was necessary that man should find out some external sensible signs, whereof those invisible ideas, which his thoughts are made up of, might be made known to others. For this purpose nothing was so fit, either for plenty or quickness, as those articulate sounds, which with so much ease and variety he found himself able to make. Thus we may conceive how *words*, which were by nature so well adapted to that purpose, came to be made use of by men as the signs of their ideas [...] But though words, as they are used by men, can properly and immediately signify nothing but the ideas that are in the mind of the speaker; yet they in their thoughts give them a secret reference to two other things.
>
> First, *They suppose their words to be marks of the ideas in the minds also of other men, with whom they communicate*: for else they should talk in vain, and could not be understood, if the

sounds they applied to one idea were such as by the hearer were applied to another, which is to speak two languages. (Locke, 1706, III, ii)

The telementation thesis is far older than Locke. It can be traced back through the modistic grammarians of the Middle Ages to Aristotle, who declares that the words we speak are 'symbols' of what he calls 'affections of the soul' (*De Interpretatione*, 1). These 'affections of the soul' correspond roughly (very roughly) to what Locke called 'ideas'. Aristotle holds that they are the same for all mankind, even though forms of speech differ from one people to another. Aristotle also holds that the external world, which is the source of our 'affections of the soul', is the same for all mankind. If we accept both of Aristotle's assumptions, it is clear that in order to communicate their thoughts to one another, members of the human race need only to agree on the same vocal 'symbols' for the same 'affections of the soul'.

On the basis of such an agreement or convention, it becomes possible in principle to set up a language. It is thus tempting to leap to the conclusion that languages are nothing other than such systems of vocal symbols, enabling human beings to communicate their thoughts in this manner; or at least that languages approximate ideally to such systems. The same supposition underlies the attempts which have been made from the seventeenth century onwards to devise a universal language. John Wilkins' 'real character' is an early example (Harris and Taylor, 1997, pp.110-125). Esperanto, invented by Zamenhof in the late nineteenth century, is perhaps the best known of these today.

In short, the Aristotelian conception of how language works is by no means dead. It survives in the notion that a language community is a group of people who have come to use the same forms of words to express or symbolize the same ideas. Communication in such a community is both telementational and determinate. That is to say, what is meant by what is said can in principle be determined, because everyone shares the same stock of ideas and the fixed code establishes the agreed correlations between the ideas and the words that symbolize or 'represent' them.

This Aristotelian version of the language myth has various corollaries which should be noted. In the first place, it dispenses with the need to suppose that any 'natural' connexion between the word and the idea is required in order to make the word an effective vocal symbol; e.g. no resemblance or mysterious affinity between the sound of the word *horse* and the speaker's concept of a horse. This corollary has survived in modern linguistics as the principle of the 'arbitrariness of the linguistic sign' (Saussure, 1922, p.100).

A further corollary is the requirement of some social mechanism to establish the convention. For whereas Aristotle's 'affections of the soul' are natural impressions derived from the external world as perceived by the senses, the vocal symbols are not. So the social mechanism becomes essential in this way of thinking about language because, as Locke points out, it would be useless for each individual, acting in isolation, to decide what sounds to use as 'marks' of ideas. This would result not in the establishment of a language, but in the establishment of Babel.

Although there is no direct connexion between Aristotle's explanation of speech and the nationalist politics of post-Renaissance Europe, it is significant that both place a considerable premium on uniformity. Deviation from the fixed code, or failure to conform to it, has undesirable consequences in both cases. The fixed code is a basic requirement of Aristotelian logic: if words can change their meanings in unforeseen ways, or have meanings unregulated by any code, the Aristotelian syllogism loses it validity. The fixed code is likewise a basic requirement for establishing a national language: if there is no public consensus as to what the 'correct' forms of speech are, the community will lack the desired common usage. In both cases a fixed code has the merit of eliminating indeterminacy and conflicts of interpretation; but only in the second case do we encounter the notion that it is the duty of the state and its institutions to impose a fixed code by fiat.

Modern versions of the language myth

A fixed code is the presumptive basis of Saussure's 'speech circuit' (see Ch. 1). For if A and B do not share a code associating the same concept with the same sound, it follows that the message eventually decoded by B will not necessarily correspond to what A originally transmitted. Other segregational theorists make the point quite explicitly. They tell us, for example, that language 'enables a speaker to transform configurations of ideas into configurations of sounds, and it enables a listener within his own mind to transform these sounds back again into a reasonable facsimile of the ideas with which the speaker began' (Chafe, 1970, p.15), and that a word is 'a shared bidirectional symbol, available to convert meaning to sound by any person when the person speaks, and sound to meaning by any person when the person listens, according to the same code' (Pinker, 1994, pp.151-2).

Thus there is a clear line of descent linking various versions of the language myth from the fourth century BC down to the late twentieth century AD. These versions differ in details and points of emphasis which need not concern us here; but all share the basic assumption that the function of a language is to supply a fixed verbal code which makes it possible for members of a given linguistic community to communicate with one another.

The model of linguistic communication we arrive at by combining a telementational theory of communication with a fixed-code theory of the system can therefore be summed up as follows:

Individuals are able to exchange their thoughts by means of words because - and insofar as - they have come to understand and to adhere to a fixed public plan for doing so. The plan is based on recurrent instantiation of invariant items belonging to a set known to all members of the community. These items are the 'sentences' of the community's language. They are invariant items in two respects: form and meaning. Knowing the forms of sentences enables those who know the language to express appropriately the thoughts they intend to convey. Knowing the meanings of sentences enables those who know the language to identify the thoughts thus expressed. Being invariant, sentences are context-free, and so proof against the vagaries of changing speakers, hearers and circumstances, rather as coin of the realm is valid irrespective of the honesty or dishonesty of individual transactions.

Thus the basic account of how human beings communicate goes like this. Suppose *A* has a thought that he wishes to communicate to *B*, for example, that gold is valuable. His task is to search among the sentences of a language known both to himself and to *B*, and select that sentence which has a meaning appropriate to the thought to be conveyed; for example, in English, the sentence *Gold is valuable*. He then encodes this sentence in its appropriate oral or written form, from which *B* is able to decode it, and in virtue of knowing what it means, grasp the thought which *A* intended to convey to him, namely that gold is valuable. (Harris, 1981a, p.10)

Some such account as this is central to what integrationists refer to as 'the language myth'; and the language myth is the foundation of segregational linguistics. The main components of the myth have their own intellectual history (Harris, 1981a), which does not call for discussion here. And the central account can be elaborated in various ways. For example, choosing the right sentence can be analysed as a process involving the handling of a complex set of procedures which select the appropriate phonemes, morphemes and syntactic constructions and fit them all together so as to 'generate' the sound-sequence required. But those details do not alter the fact that in the end we are dealing with a simple bi-planar code in which 'forms' are paired with 'meanings' and the linguistic sign is itself a determinate bi-planar pairing of this type.

Phonology, morphology, syntax and semantics can all be fitted in to the same bi-planar model; and this is doubtless one reason for the powerful hold that the language myth still has on contemporary linguistics. Another reason is it is a myth that always lends itself to convenient restatement in accordance with the latest fashionable terminology. Here, for example, is a generativist version of the mid-1960s:

> A linguistic description of a natural language is an attempt to reveal the nature of a fluent speaker's mastery of that language. This mastery is manifested in the speaker's ability to communicate with other speakers of the language: to produce appropriate sentences that convey information, ask questions, give commands, etc., and to understand the sentences of other speakers. Thus a linguistic description must reconstruct the principles underlying the ability of speakers to communicate with one another. Such a reconstruction is a scientific theory whose statements represent the linguistic structure characteristic of the language and whose deductive consequences enable the linguist to explain sentence use and comprehension in terms of features of this structure. (Katz and Postal, 1964, p.1)

The authors go on to argue that such a description must contain three parts or components: a syntactic component, a semantic component and a phonological component. Their explanation continues as follows:

> In such a tripartite theory of linguistic descriptions, certain psychological claims are made about the speaker's capacity to communicate fluently. The fundamental claim is that the fluent speaker's ability to use and understand speech involves a basic mechanism that enables him to construct the formal syntactic structures underlying the sentences which these utterances represent, and two subsidiary mechanisms: one that associates a set of meanings with each formal syntactic structure and another that maps such structures into phonetic representations, which are, in turn, the input to his speech apparatus. (Katz and Postal, 1964, p.2)

Saussure would never have described his programme in such terms as these. Nevertheless, the language myth is recognizably the same in 1964 as it was when Saussure died. What is postulated is the existence of a fixed code of bi-planar pairings between forms and meanings. It is access to this code which allows speaker and hearer to communicate; and communication in turn is envisaged as a process of telementation. The only difference between Katz and Postal's model and Saussure's concerns the structure of the code. In Katz and Postal's model the connexions between form and meaning are mediated by the syntactic component. No such component is recognized by Saussure. But far from disowning Saussure's theoretical framework, Katz and Postal argue that their conception of the relationship between linguistic form and linguistic meaning actually supports Saussure's. Concerning their tri-partite model, they write:

> This characteristic of linguistic descriptions is the formal analogue of Saussure's dictum that the connection between form and meaning is arbitrary. Moreover, the arbitrariness of this connection can be *explained* in terms of the fact that the semantic and phonological components perform independent operations on different features of the syntactic output. (Katz and Postal, 1964, p.2)

In other words, whereas Saussure had simply *assumed* that a fixed code somehow supplied arbitrary connections between sound and sense, Katz and Postal offer a fixed code where that is a necessary consequence of the way the code is broken down into its component parts. Indeed, that is why knowledge of the same code is so essential for communication between speaker and hearer. Without it, there would be no way of guessing what the pairings of form and meaning are.

A more recent endorsement of the language myth is the version given by Pinker in his book *The Language Instinct.* According to Pinker, grammar is a 'form of mental software' that the brain has evolved over countless generations. Why was this necessary? Because, says Pinker, the human ear, the human mouth and the human mind are 'three very different kinds of machine'. Grammar interconnects them. These, again, are terms Saussure would never have used – in particular the computer analogy. But the story Pinker tells is clearly recognizable as yet another version of the language myth. The new twist in Pinker's version is that underlying the language we speak there is another kind of language called 'mentalese'. It is this underlying language that supplies the meanings for the words and sentences of the language we actually speak. These meanings are what Pinker calls 'chunks of mentalese'. What we have to do when we speak English, or French, or any other language is translate *from* mentalese *into* English, or French, or whatever language it may be. We are not usually aware of doing this translation, but the reason why we have to do it, according to Pinker, is that we do not think in our native language at all, but in mentalese. The actual languages we speak for everyday purposes are very imperfect instruments for expressing our thoughts. Pinker writes:

> The representations underlying thinking, on the one hand, and the sentences in a language, on the other, are in many ways at cross purposes. (Pinker, 1994, p.81)

He does not explain how he thinks this disastrous evolutionary mismatch has come about, but he continues:

> Any particular thought in our head embraces a vast amount of information. But when it comes to communicating a thought to someone else, attention spans are short and mouths are slow. To get information into a listener's head in a reasonable amount of time, a speaker can encode only a fraction of the message into words and must count on the listener to fill in the rest. (Pinker, 1994, p.81)

From this it is clear that Pinker is just as much committed as Saussure to the doctrine of telementation. Communication is, or aims at, thought transference. He is also, like Saussure, committed to the doctrine of languages as fixed codes. Like all generativists, he distinguishes between 'grammatical' and 'ungrammatical' combinations of words, and he explains what he takes to be our ability to recognize ungrammatical combinations in the following terms: 'Ungrammaticality is simply a consequence of our having a fixed code for interpreting sentences' (Pinker, 1994, p.88). He draws an explicit analogy between this fixed code and that used by computers to detect errors in input signals. In short, what we find in Pinker is the language myth dressed up in the fashionable garb of computerspeak.

The historical significance of all this should not be overlooked. Pinker's book was published 80 years after Saussure's death, and modern linguistics had undergone a number of self-proclaimed revolutions in the interim. But in spite of all that, what emerges in the 1990s is the same basic story that had been proposed in the early 1900s. In orthodox linguistics there has been no theoretical advance, but merely a succession of formal refinements to one traditional model.

Integrational linguistics and demythologization

A linguistics based on this myth will automatically assume that the linguist's first task in coming to terms with the speech of any monoglot linguistic community is to identify 'the system' (i.e. the underlying fixed code) that is in use and to analyse it as completely and carefully as possible. In other words, 'the language' of this community is implicitly taken to be not only available to the linguist as an object of description, but one which must be described in some detail before further investigation of what goes on in the conduct of linguistic communication can be undertaken. This seems, at first sight, no less reasonable than saying that if we wish to investigate the way business is carried out in a given society, we first need an account of the currency system in use. In both cases 'the system' is assumed to exist as some kind of autonomous organization which exists over and above the particular transactions it facilitates.

The next question in the linguistic case is: how does the linguist gain access to information about 'the system' (i.e. the language)? The notion that one might obtain this information simply by asking the users (as one might, for example, hope to gain basic information about the currency of a country simply by going to a market or a bank and making inquiries) is usually regarded by professional linguists as naive and mistaken. The assumption here is that although speakers of a language are perfectly accustomed to using the system, it is too complex for them to have any detached intellectual grasp of its structure. Even when asked about specific details (such as the meaning of a particular word or the synonymy of two or more forms), the ordinary speaker's reply is regarded as unreliable for purposes of linguistics (Bloomfield, 1935, p.160). Curiously, however, the same speaker's judgment as to whether a combination of forms is 'grammatical' or 'ungrammatical' is often regarded as well-nigh infallible; or, at least, as providing the ultimate evidence on which the linguist can count. These methodological difficulties are the inevitable consequences of a language myth which projects an unobservable 'system' as the basis of observable linguistic behaviour. This generates an initial problem about eliciting and gathering the relevant information (quite apart from the further problem of what is done with the information once it is gathered).

Faith in information-gathering was one of the hallmarks of nineteenth-century positivist science, and it had a profound influence on the development of modern linguistics. During the twentieth century positivism has declined in most areas of the humanities, as more and more scholars came to realize its bankruptcy as an intellectual creed. Orthodox linguistics, however, remained one of the last strongholds of positivism: it might even be said to be one of the few academic areas in the humanities where positivism gained ground. (That gain is particularly notable in what is now known as 'sociolinguistics', where tables of statistics, graphs and other forms of number-crunching are still obligatory indicators of 'research'.)

From an integrational perspective, it is just as naive to suppose that gathering and collating 'data' about linguistic forms and their occurrence will automatically lead to enlightenment about fundamental questions concerning language as to suppose that collecting coins and noting their provenance will eventually result in an understanding of buying and selling. On the contrary, a focus on collecting information is more likely to divert attention from the basic questions that need to be addressed. Students are thus misled into thinking that there is an endless reservoir of linguistic facts 'out there', waiting to be collected by any boy scout with the right collecting equipment. (On the integrationist view of 'linguistic facts', see Ch. 6.) What is of great interest to anyone making a serious study of the intellectual history of the modern world is how this form of positivism could have taken root so deeply in language studies. And the short answer an integrationist will give is that its source is the orthodox belief in the traditional Western language myth, i.e. in the existence of autonomous systems called 'languages', concerning which information can be compiled by observational techniques no different in principle from those employed in geology or ornithology.

Integrational linguistics is sometimes described as being or as promoting a 'demythologized' linguistics. What this implies is certainly an abandonment of the language myth in any of the versions described above. But various possible grounds for this rejection need to be distinguished.

(1) It might be claimed that linguistics must abandon the language myth because the notion of a public fixed code which reliably enables members of the community to exchange their thoughts fails to correspond to any observable linguistic reality. In other words, there just is no such thing as 'a language' in this sense: linguistic usage never being uniform, but manifestly diverse and variable, even among members of quite small communities, let alone in communities with millions of members. So a linguistics based on the language myth (in any of its various forms) is as inadequate as an economics based on the assumption that all members of society behave in an economically uniform way. Whatever the reason for making the assumption, it simply does not fit our experience of linguistic behaviour. If linguistics is to be taken seriously, the argument would run, it needs a more plausible model.

Segregationists often construe this as being the main integrationist objection to the language myth and respond to it as follows. A language (*qua* 'system') does not require absolute uniformity of practice, but only reasonable similarity, in order to function as an effective means of communication. Provided the system is fairly stable, it will work. In short, a certain amount of variation is not only tolerable but perfectly compatible with the notion of a fixed code shared by all members of the community.

In reply to this, an integrationist might point out that making this move does nothing at all to rescue the credibility of the language myth. For if the segregationist hypothesis allows A and B to differ systematically in respect of the way in which each uses sounds to express concepts, then either communication between them will break down (i.e. they do not in fact share a common code), or else it must be the case that there are two codes in operation and each understands both. In other words, this is a solution which salvages the language myth by multiplying fixed codes. And that merely displaces the problem, as well as making it worse. For the segregationist now has to make sense of the notion of communication *across* codes – which defeats the object of appealing to a fixed code in the first place.

It makes no more sense for the fixed-code theorist to claim that fixed codes require only 'approximate' systematization than it would for the

Bank of England to declare that there are only 'approximately' one hundred pence to a pound. If *A* traded on the assumption that there were ninety-nine pence to a pound, while *B* traded on the assumption that there were a hundred and one, they would soon come to blows. The whole point of having a fixed system (either of speech or of currency) is presumably to eliminate such discrepancies: to allow them is already to admit that the system is *not* fixed. (For discussion of a related misconception of linguistic determinacy, see Ch. 6)

(2) A more robust integrationist case for rejecting the language myth runs as follows. Irrespective of whether there actually are any linguistic communities using a language which conforms to the hypothetical criteria for fixed codes, the problem with a fixed-code model is that it begs precisely those questions that linguistic inquiry should be trying to answer. How do we in practice assess what other people mean by what they say? How do we judge that verbal communication has been successful? Or unsuccessful? How do we measure our own proficiency in linguistic communication? Do we always know what we mean? What role does the perception of apparent linguistic similarities and differences play in our construction of the linguistic world in which we live? The facile appeal to fixed codes as a basis for communication does nothing to throw light on any of these questions. Even less does it illuminate such fundamental matters as our apparent ability to change our linguistic practices, to extend them creatively, to devise new forms of exploiting language, to transpose from one medium to another.

(3) A third ground for rejecting the fixed code as a linguistic model concerns the ontogeny of the model itself. Manifestly, it is a theoretical abstraction arrived at by suppressing as many dimensions of variation as possible: in particular, variations in what integrationists regard as the unavoidable biomechanical, macrosocial and circumstantial parameters of communication (see Ch.1). The result is that one deliberately simplified artificial construct comes to be proposed as a basis for explaining everything else. This is sometimes defended by segregationists as a 'necessary idealization' (see pp.58-9) essential to 'scientific' analysis. But it is more like proposing that the black-and-white photograph be taken as a model of what the eye actually sees. The demythologization that integrational linguistics proposes starts not from any convenient reduction of complexity but, on the contrary, by allowing that language may be no less complex than the individual circumstances of which particular linguistic episodes are the product. In short, integrationism recognizes no limit to what might – or might not – be pertinent to linguistic communication in specific cases. But since *every episode of linguistic communication is a specific case*, the notion of linguistic inquiry as a segregated or segregatable domain of inquiry immediately collapses. And the attraction of appealing to fixed codes along with it.

From an integrational point of view, therefore, to adopt or adapt some version of the language myth as a theoretical basis for linguistics amounts to tackling the whole range of linguistic problems from the wrong end, and in a manner which will inevitably generate bogus problems as to whether people are speaking 'the same language' or not.

Languages in history

The notion of a language as a fixed code also comes into conflict with the notion that languages are subject to change over periods of time. No one who had tried to read both Chaucer's *Canterbury Tales* and Orwell's *Animal Farm* could fail to notice some obvious linguistic disparities. Being able to read and understand the latter is no guarantee of being able to read and understand the former. Nevertheless, many are prepared not only to call both of them 'English' texts but to say that they are texts in 'the same language' in spite of their disparities.

In modern linguistics, the solution usually adopted is to insist on an absolute distinction between **'synchronic'** and **'diachronic'** linguistics. The terms are Saussure's (Saussure, 1922, p. 117) but they have passed into general currency among linguists. The language as a fixed code is then identified as a synchronic concept, while the language as a historically evolving continuum is identified as a diachronic concept. With this distinction in place, there is supposedly no longer any contradiction between saying on the one hand that Chaucer's English is quite a different language from Orwell's English (two separate synchronic systems) and on the other that Orwell's English and Chaucer's are the same language (part of a single diachronic continuum).

The integrationist will point out that, far from resolving the contradiction, this metalinguistic manœuvre makes it worse. What it does is try to draw a distinction between two applications of the term 'language', from one of which the passage of time is by definition excluded. But that is a clear case of grabbing the wrong sow by the ear. It is not by discounting the passage of time that you validate the notion of different linguistic systems; nor by appealing to temporal continuity that you can discount linguistic differences. All linguistic communication, for the integrationist, is time-bound. There is no sense in which the sounds, the words or whatever was said survive over time, other than by being remembered, repeated or recorded. Statements linking or equating linguistic items across a gap of generations or of centuries (of the kind typically encountered in manuals of historical linguistics) are, for the integrationist, products of a second-order metalanguage with theoretical credentials of an extremely questionable kind. The development of this metalanguage (particularly from the beginning of the nineteenth century) is itself an interesting topic for linguistic investigation, but to accept it *ab initio* as capturing a certain order of linguistic 'facts' would be a theoretical move quite incompatible with an integrational approach to language.

For here we see the manufacture of a complementary language myth to supplement the segregationist's fixed-code doctrine: this is a myth about a mysterious linguistic object which remains the same while changing all the time. The more clear-sighted theorists of diachronic linguistics actually realize the difficulty, but try to finesse it in various ways. Saussure's embarrassment over the notion of diachronic identity is well known (Love, 1984; Harris, 1987b, pp.162-166). Bolder attempts to cut the Gordian knot include simply elevating the occurrence of linguistic change into a kind of super-axiom. Labov, for instance, sets out his stall as a theorist of diachronic linguistics by declaring:

> The *fact* of language change is a given; it is too obvious to be recorded or even listed among the assumptions of our research. (Labov, 1994, p.9)

The claim is nothing if not enigmatic. For it is difficult to see what could possibly count as 'recording' the fact of language change. And if it is too obvious to mention, why mention it? There are signs here of a deep embarrassment akin to Saussure's. In both cases the cause of the embarrassment is not hard to spot: it is that, contrary to the bluff reassurances of the orthodox linguist, language change *cannot* be observed and is *not* a 'fact'. It is a hypothesis, and one with a very curious empirical basis. What *can* be observed are not changes but differences; and their observation has a temporal dimension. But that is quite a different matter (as Saussure clearly saw) from claiming that there is 'something' that has undergone a change. For the 'something' in this instance is a theoretical abstraction. And it is an abstraction that the integrationist sees no case for accepting, other than a purely 'hocus-pocus' case. But, to repeat a point made earlier, integrationists are not hocus-pocus linguists.

What is interesting from an integrational point of view is the role that this abstraction plays in the rationale of orthodox linguistics. The bits and pieces of language that mysteriously change while remaining the same (the words that can change both form and meaning while nevertheless retaining their own historical identity) are not just ghosts in the diachronic machine. They also serve a purpose in validating the postulation of a synchronic fixed code. This is perhaps most clearly revealed in Saussure's illuminating comparison of a language with a plant. A longitudinal section of the stem corresponds to diachronic linguistics, while a cross-cut corresponds to synchronic linguistics. The point is that although the patterns revealed to the observer by the longitudinal cut and the cross-cut are different patterns, they are connected. And not just contingently: we are told quite explicitly that the synchronic and the diachronic are 'interdependent'. The synchronic perspective simply shows a different view of the same linguistic 'fibres' that the diachronic perspective reveals 'longitudinally' (Saussure, 1922, pp.124-5). This botanic comparison, clearly, would make no sense at all unless we were supposed to understand *both* patterns as resulting from the continous growth over time of a single organic entity. For that is what ensures that *wherever* the stem is cut horizontally what is revealed is an organized pattern, and not just a chaotic jumble. In other words, at no point in time, supposedly, is the linguistic community ever *without* a synchronic fixed code.

But the diachronic pattern, as Saussure concedes, is not in fact available to the ordinary language-user. It is revealed only to the historical hindsight of the linguist. That is why in synchronic linguistics the linguist must make every effort to 'suppress the past' (Saussure, 1922, p.177). How we can be sure that the diachronic linguist has 20-20 hindsight Saussure does not explain. And there is no independent 'psychological reality' to report in this domain. We seem to be left with linguists reporting their own retrospections. It is as close as Saussure ever comes to admitting that diachronic linguistics may be hocus-pocus.

The dialect myth

Another common segregational strategy for reconciling fixed codes on the one hand with linguistic variation on the other is to appeal to the notion of 'dialects'. This makes it more plausible – superficially, at least – to maintain that 'the same language' is spoken throughout a certain population, while admitting that it is spoken differently by different groups within that population. In short, the function of the dialect myth in orthodox linguistics is to provide theoretical support for the idea that there can be linguistic unity in diversity. The dialect is thus identified as 'the system' constituting the immediate object of the linguist's description, and a language is construed (either synchronically or diachronically) as a set of dialects. It follows that a description of 'the language' simply *is* the description of its various dialects.

Traditionally, dialects were supposed to have a geographical basis, varying from one locality to another, but more recently the term 'dialect' has often been extended by linguists to the social as well as the regional distribution of linguistic features. A more general term which leaves open whether the distribution is social, regional or has any other basis is 'variety'.

The history of the notion 'dialect' is long and chequered. The word itself is said to go back to the Greek *dialektos*, although the Greek writers of antiquity often do not seem particularly concerned to draw a clear distinction between dialects and languages. They were, however, aware of variations in Greek usage between one Greek community and another, recognizing 'the same word' in characteristically different but not totally unrelated spoken (and written) forms. The recognition of such correspondences, all the more prominent if certain types of difference tend to go together, is doubtless the primitive basis of lay distinctions between one regional dialect and another. It affords a ground for saying that the speech of some neighbouring community is not (quite) the same as the speech of one's own community. It also sets up a paradigm for mimicking that other form of speech (often for purposes of ridicule).

If this account of the origin of the concept of dialects is on the right lines, it is plausible to suppose that the limits of that lay concept are reached when linguistic differences between the speech of one community and the speech of another are too great to permit intercomprehension. For then there is no basis for recognizing 'the same word' in variant forms. In short, dialects emerge as varieties of speech which, although characteristically different, are not so divergent as to prevent linguistic communication of some kind between speakers of one and speakers of another. It is in this sense that the lay person may be willing, for instance, to count a Londoner and a New Yorker as speaking 'the same language' (English) while acknowledging the very considerable differences in the English they speak.

In orthodox linguistics, however, the concept of a dialect has been given a quite different interpretation or interpretations. One of these imposes a historical dimension on the concept. Thus the criterion of dialectal relationship becomes not whether or not speakers of two linguistic varieties can understand one another and recognize regular parallels between their forms of speech, but whether or not the varieties in question are historically derived from a common ancestor. (Thus Greek and Latin may be referred to as 'dialects' of Indo-European, assuming that in fact there originally was at some time in the past a single language from which the historically attested forms of Greek and Latin are descended.) The question of what 'proves' historical descent is contentious, but for present purposes can be left on one side.

A quite different interpretation of the concept in modern linguistics is given by Bloch's famous definition of a dialect as 'a class of idiolects with the same phonological system' (Bloch, 1948, pp.7-8). What is important here is not the qualification 'with the same phonological system' (for this already raises more problems than it solves) but the notion that a dialect can be defined as a collection of individual forms of speech grouped together. (The definition is bizarre in that it apparently allows for a dialect of which the speakers might be quite unable to understand one another.) An idiolect, for Bloch, is 'the totality of the possible utterances of one speaker at one time in using a language to interact with one other speaker'. Again, we do not need to probe the obscurities of this sibylline formula to grasp that what the definition does is take the speech of the individual as the basic variable and define the dialect by classifying individuals together in some way in respect of the 'sameness' of their speech.

The integrationist rejects both these interpretations of what a dialect is. In both cases the identity of 'the language' is tacitly taken as given (as a diachronic postulate in one case and a synchronic postulate in the other) and then used as a basis for distinguishing types and degrees of variation. But this is a manœuvre which leads straight back to reinstating the fixed code as a *sine qua non* in discussing language. The result is a dialect myth in which dialects are themselves construed as fixed codes, but differing in such a way as to allow them to stand as variants or subcodes in virtue of their relationship to some archetype. Whereas what linguistics needs, in the integrationist's view, is a framework for examining linguistic diversity which does *not* presuppose that it must always be discussed by reference to some prior concept of linguistic unity. It is the concept of linguistic unity which is theoretically problematic; not the concept of linguistic diversity.

A version of the dialect myth of particular interest to integrationists is that which distinguishes sharply between 'dialect' and 'accent'. This is very popular with British sociolinguists, but perhaps less so with British dialect speakers themselves. The effect, clearly, is to allow that the same fixed code (= 'dialect') can be spoken, in theory at least, with any one of a number of different forms of pronunciation (= 'accent'), thus retaining its identity in diversity. *Plus ça change, plus c'est la même chose.*

The myth of 'standard' languages

For many linguists, the term 'dialect' contrasts with 'standard', and dialect pronunciations, words, syntax, etc. are said to be **'non-standard'** (or sometimes 'sub-standard'). But what is a standard language or standard usage supposed to be?

Varying and by no means consistent accounts of this are given in orthodox linguistics, but the integrationist regards them all with suspicion for a number of reasons. One is that a common thread running through the orthodox definitions is an appeal to the notion of superiority or 'prestige', as it is often called; but is unclear whether the prestige attaches to the speakers or what they speak. The phrase 'prestige variety' is ambiguous as between these two very different concepts. It is also unclear how this prestige is measured. Thus when we encounter what appears at first sight to be a bold and uncompromising statement of sociolinguistic 'fact', such as 'the most prestigious British dialect is standard English' (Hughes and Trudgill, 1979, p.12), it is often difficult to work out exactly what is being asserted. Who are the judges in the prestige stakes? Do they regard themselves as speakers of standard English? And how many other dialects are they acquainted with? (For this way of stating the assessment already assumes that standard English is itself a dialect, but only one among many.) Furthermore, what value is to be attached to such judgments if it is the case, as some linguists say, that 'they are almost always made in ignorance of the nature of dialect and how it relates to the standard language' (O'Donnell and Todd, 1980, p.17)?

Related problems attach to unpacking the definition to be found in the *Oxford English Dictionary* (1933 Supplement), which describes the term 'standard' as 'applied to the variety of the speech of a country which, by reason of its cultural status and currency, is held to represent the best form of that speech'. Here at least it is clear that the value judgment attaches, allegedly, to the speech and not to the speakers. But the reasons given for the judgment are puzzling. Do 'cultural status' and 'currency' go together? Is it being implied that 'standard' speech enjoys greater currency than non-standard? If so, it is difficult to square with the assertions of linguists who tell us that standard English is spoken only by a minority of the English-speaking population, and even that most speakers of standard English include some non-standard features in their speech.

The plausibility of the idea that a standard language exists is connected in obvious ways to the possibility of pointing to some codification of it (such as grammar books and dictionaries provide). But grammarians and lexicographers, along with language 'academies', tend to regard themselves as authorities on, guardians of, or even arbiters of linguistic 'correctness'. And here we come to another reason for treating the notion of a 'standard' language with caution: the common equation of 'standard' with 'correct' and 'non-standard' with 'incorrect'. Those who tell us that modern linguistics is descriptive not prescriptive shift uncomfortably from one foot to the other when dealing with these equations and their pedagogic implications. They try to maintain that no dialect and indeed no current linguistic forms of any kind are 'in themselves' more correct than others, but this leaves the alleged 'prestige' of the standard language in a kind of irrational limbo. The way out of the limbo is often an appeal to the notion of 'appropriateness'. Thus, for instance, when comparing 'the person to whom I wrote' to 'the chap I wrote to', it will be claimed that one phrase 'is not more correct than the other' and 'the word *chap* is in no way inferior to the word *person*' (Hughes and Trudgill, 1979, p.10). Likewise, 'swear words and slang are not wrong in themselves'. So why do schools discourage their pupils from using them? It is all, Hughes and Trudgill tell us, 'a matter not of correctness but of appropriateness'. The subtlety is one which presumably passes over the heads of most pupils and doubtless many of their teachers. What would standard English be if not the kind of English that is appropriate if you want your English to sound 'correct'?

The fudge introduced by implying that an objective distinction can be drawn between 'appropriate' and 'correct' is compounded when we are told that standard English is 'not the dialect of any social group, but of educated people throughout the British Isles' (Hughes and Trudgill, 1979, p.10). Why 'educated people' do not count as a 'social group' is left unexplained, as is the question of exactly how educated you have to be to be sure that your English is standard. Since education in Britain has been compulsory since Disraeli's Act of 1876, it might seem to follow that virtually the entire population now speaks standard English. But it seems doubtful whether that is what the sociolinguists are trying to tell us.

A third kind of doubt about the notion 'standard' arises when we observe the ease with which, in orthodox linguistics, standards seem to multiply. Thus we find linguists distinguishing not only 'standard British English' from 'standard American English', but from 'standard Australian English', 'standard New Zealand English', 'standard Scottish English', 'standard English English' and so on. One even encounters 'standard standard English'. It is difficult to see where this multiplication of standards stops, or why any dialect cannot, in principle, have its own standard. But since all these standards differ one from another, even if only in minor details, their proliferation in the end simply renders the notion 'standard' self-stultifying. We are back on the familiar terrain of dialect variation.

In all these cases one sees orthodox linguistics desperately seeking to rescue the doctrine that 'languages' *qua* codes actually exist as observable social practices, irrespective of their users' beliefs about them – in the face of a challenge from the notion that 'making value judgements on language is an integral part of using it' (Cameron, 1995, p.3).

The idiolect myth

One further segregationist manœuvre must be mentioned here. Relocating the fixed code at the level of dialects rather than at the level of languages still leaves open the possibility that not all speakers of a given dialect will speak it in exactly the same way. One way of dealing with this (the distinction between dialect and accent) has already been mentioned. But it is not uncommon for linguists to claim that 'however narrowly we define the speech community, by geographical and social criteria, we shall always find a certain degree of systematic variation in the speech of its members' (Lyons, 1970, p.19). Segregationists anxious to eliminate this ultimate problem of subdialectal variation have consequently been driven to relocate the fixed code at a lower level still, and identified the 'idiolect' of each individual speaker as their object of description (and the ultimate 'system' on which linguistic communication is based).

Exactly how the idiolect is to be defined is a matter of controversy among segregationists, but a more important point for our present purposes is that, however it is defined, the identification of the 'system' with the individual resurrects the problem of explaining how *A* communicates with *B* if each is using *ex hypothesi* a different code. For successful communication would then seem to depend on good luck, i.e. the chance 'overlap' between *A*'s system and *B*'s, each being in principle independent. (This problem was evident to Saussure, who consequently makes a point of refusing to allow that the community's language system (*la langue*) could be complete in any one individual. In other words, he rejects the idiolect as the linguist's object of description.) Quite apart from this, however, there is the no less serious problem posed by the fact that the very notion of an idiolect seems to imply that the individual constantly speaks in a characteristic and uniform way. That this is far from being the case is suggested not only by personal experience but by studies documenting the phenomenon called 'accommodation', whereby speakers consciously or unconsciously adapt the way they speak towards that of their interlocutors (Coupland and Giles, 1988).

Thus the whole problem with the notion 'idiolect' is that it is conjured up by a purely segregationist dilemma: how to draw a line on the slippery slope between the macrosocial and the circumstantial (as an integrationist would put it). The solution, which varies with different segregational theorists, consists in arbitrarily selecting certain circumstantial criteria and declaring that on one side of a dividing line demarcated by those criteria variation is 'linguistic', but on the other side 'non-linguistic'. This, an integrationist will submit, is a purely hocus-pocus way out: it corresponds to no communicational 'reality' either for the individual or for the community.

It is also worth noting here that the point at which the theoretical concept of the idiolect is introduced is also the point at which synchronic and diachronic linguistics ultimately part company. In other words, while it makes some kind of sense to say that languages or dialects can be passed on from one generation of speakers to the next, this make no sense at all in the case of idiolects, since by definition the idiolect belongs to one individual only. It dies with that person. So if languages are in the final analysis idiolectal, they are dying out at a phenomenal rate; much faster than the most gloomy calculations suggest.

Sometimes the postulation of a single 'standard language' for the community and the postulation of 'idiolects' for all its members are run in tandem, as if they were alternatives or equivalents. And at least in one respect they are. For treating 'the system' as something located inside the speaker's head is another way of reinstating the doctrine of the fixed code. But re-identifying 'the language' as the individual's personal system will not eliminate variation or inconsistency unless it is assumed that the individual's linguistic behaviour is actually bound by it. The idiolect must not be modified or compromised when speaking to others who *ex hypothesi* have different idiolects. What also has to be precluded is the possibility that the idiolect may change over time (which includes from one utterance to the next). In other words, there would be no point in shifting the linguistic object to be described from community to individual if it were assumed that individuals could depart from their own idiolects in practice. For then there would still be language not explicable by reference to the code. And that is exactly what the hypothesis of the completely homogeneous community is also designed to preclude.

The status of 'languages'

The question of the status of 'languages' *qua* systems is a useful point of departure for comparing the integrational and segregational approaches, although it will already be apparent from what has been said above that the differences between them go much deeper than this single issue. Nevertheless, it is a crucial issue for various reasons. Although, as already mentioned, linguists such as Sapir, Malinowski, Pike and Firth were clearly unhappy with certain aspects of segregationist thinking, it never seems to have struck them that there was any theoretical room within linguistics for presenting a distinct alternative view of this status. They did not, apparently, regard this as a fundamental question. Consequently they failed to present linguistics with the kind of challenge that integrationism now offers.

This challenge may be put in the form of the following proposition: *linguistic analysis does not require the assumption that there are languages.*

A more explicit formulation would be the following:

> it is possible to do linguistics without assuming that the linguistic universe consists of a large number of discrete objects called 'languages', let alone having to treat each such object as a self-contained system. (Harris, 1998b)

Since it is exactly the opposite assumption which underlies the terms in which orthodox linguistics has always presented its programme – as well as its claim to be an independent academic discipline – the clear implication of the integrationist challenge is that something in modern linguistics went very wrong somewhere. Where exactly? Right at the beginning, according to the integrationist. The theorists of modern linguistics made the mistake of deciding to treat languages as autonomous first-order objects in their own right: in other words, to treat every language as a 'given'. Each such object was assumed to lead an existence of its own, to have its own origin, its own history, its own speakers, its own writing system in ceratin cases, and therefore to be available for investigation and description, preferably by the 'scientific' methods which the discipline of linguistics would spell out. Above all, each such language was 'given' as recognizably different from all others. Saussure, the most lucid of all segregational theorists, made this clear when he said: 'Pour la linguistique, c'est bien le fait primordial que la diversité des langues.' ('As far as linguistics is concerned, the diversity of languages is indeed the fundamental fact.' Komatsu and Harris, 1993, p.12.) But what this boils down to is that, for orthodox linguistics, languages are objects identified by theoretical hypostatization. That act of theoretical hypostatization is what the integrationist both rejects and denies to be necessary.

The difference between integrationist and segregationist may not at first seem to be of major importance when stated in these terms. Neither denies that, for instance, many people today regard themselves as speaking English; regard the English language as separate from French, German, etc. The difference would initially appear to be that the integrationist is cautiously non-committal as to how far this 'second-order construct' called *English* corresponds to anything 'real' in linguistic behaviour; whereas the segregationist assumes that it fairly obviously does, and that *what* it corresponds to is objectively describable.

However, some orthodox linguists would go further. They would say that the 'second-order construct' is quite irrelevant, because the English language *does* exist, and is describable, irrespective of what its speakers happen to *believe* about it. And, by the same token, irrespective of what 'second-order constructs' it might give rise to. They would further maintain that it is very important for linguists not to confuse describing linguistic facts with describing linguistic beliefs; and that language description is concerned with the former, not the latter. (Let us call this the 'ontologically tough' position on languages. It is sometimes confused with the 'God's-truth' position; but in principle it is possible to be a God's-truth linguist and nevertheless be sceptical about the existence of languages.)

This now makes the difference between integrationist and segregationist seem somewhat more substantial. But the difference is wider still. One major consequence of adopting a segregationist position in orthodox linguistics, whether 'ontologically tough' or otherwise, was the establishment of an implicit order of priority among certain metalinguistic questions. Thus, for instance, it was assumed that a question such as 'Who are the speakers of Kalaba?' cannot be answered *before* the question 'What is Kalaba?' has been answered. In other words, the linguistic community was defined by reference to the hypostatized linguistic object, not vice versa.

The myth of the 'native speaker'

This is a crucial move in the orthodox strategy for linguistic description, and it would be difficult to exaggerate its importance. Although it might seem to be a theoretical matter of interest only to linguists, that is far from being the case. It has quite significant social and political implications. What it does is confer a privileged status on certain members of the linguistic community. These are the people who have been born and brought up under the 'right' conditions; namely, brought up to speak the language from birth in a family where the parents or other adults were also brought up to speak the language from birth. Such people are often referred to by orthodox linguists as 'native speakers' of the language, although the precise definition of this term is disputed. (For a sceptical account, see Paikeday, 1985.) In this way, a potential ranking is established among actual members of a linguistic community, i.e. among 'real live' individuals, as distinct from hypothetical figures in utopian linguistics. This ranking in practice reflects the utility to the linguist of particular persons as potential 'informants'. At the top come the native speakers. Next will come those who are almost native speakers, but not quite. Then will come those who did not learn the language until adulthood. And so on. On the fringes of the community will be the hangers-on, those whose command of the language is poor or suspect (typically recent immigrants, foreign workers, etc.).

The notion also has implications for the ranking of linguistic communities themselves. It is the monoglot community which the language myth projects as the 'normal' case. (Significantly, in Saussure's *Cours* there is not a single mention of bilingualism, even though Saussure was Swiss.) Communities in which two or more languages are spoken, and in which various forms of so-called 'language interference' are rife, are clearly difficult to deal with in terms of fixed-code models. Even more 'abnormal' on this scale of comparison will be linguistic communities which lack 'native speakers' altogether. (The languages spoken in such cases are referred to technically in orthodox linguistics as 'pidgins', a term with scarcely veiled connotations of inadequacy and inferiority. One authority on the subject, while protesting that 'there is no such thing as a primitive or inferior language', nevertheless feels obliged to define a pidgin as 'a marginal language which arises to fulfil certain restricted communication needs among people who have no common language': Todd, 1974, p.1. In short, not a 'proper' language.)

What is evident enough in all this is that the principal desideratum from the orthodox linguist's point of view is that the language the 'native speaker' speaks shall be 'pure', uncontaminated by any external linguistic influences. This concern is supposedly motivated by scruples akin to those in the physical sciences, where it is often important that only unadulterated samples are subject to analysis, for fear of producing unreliable results. However, it is no coincidence that 'purity' features as an important concept in many totalitarian systems of thought, as well as being reflected in linguistic legislation of a plainly chauvinistic character (such as that in force in parts of Canada and the recent *loi Toubon* enacted in France, not to mention current attempts to 'Croatize' Croatian – a policy with clear links to that of 'ethnic cleansing' in the former Jugoslavia). This, for the integrationist, demonstrates how naive it would be to suppose that the language myth – and the segregational linguistics based upon it – can be considered ideologically neutral.

Languages and linguistic behaviour

For the segregationist, actual speech (*parole* in Saussurean terminology, *performance* in generativist terminology) already *is* the use of *a* language. This is not so for the integrationist. Speech has quite a different status. The integrationist 'starts from the premise that communication proceeds by means of signs which are created at and for the moment of communicational exchange' (Wolf and Love, 1993, p.313). This will strike many educated Western people as a surprising and even a perverse claim. Why? Because they are accustomed to thinking that most of the words they use in their daily communicational exchanges were not created on the spot, but have been in existence for quite a long time. And that in turn is part of their belief that the language they speak has a history. What this shows, according to the integrationist, is the power of the second-order construct (their notion of 'the language') in shaping people's perceptions of their own first-order linguistic behaviour (their speech). The linguist, in the integrationist's view, would be ill-advised to discount this, but no less ill-advised to take it at face value. In other words, people's interpretations of their own linguistic behaviour must not necessarily be assumed to be right (any more than their interpretations of their own behaviour in general should be assumed to be right). On the other hand, nor should linguists assume that the linguist stands professionally 'outside' such questions and is in a position to provide a better assessment of linguistic behaviour than the speakers themselves.

A somewhat fuller formulation of the integrationist premise may be given as follows:

> The context of the linguistic act, which includes the assumptions the speaker may hold about the hearer's intentions,...creates the sign. The linguistic sign is not given in advance of the situation. (Davis, H.G., 1990, p.9)

The important point here is that focussing on the familiarity of 'the words' used (seeing them primarily as items recognizable from countless previous occasions, or as items already recorded in the dictionary) involves a significant shift away from the speaker's or the hearer's *immediate* perspective. It amounts to a decontextualization in which the particularity of the linguistic act is already lost, or on the way to being lost.

The decontextualization involved is rather like supposing that when you are personally involved in a road accident your first concern is with whether such a thing has ever happened to anyone else. No: your first concern is with *these* injuries, *these* responsibilities, *these* consequences. Not with the statistics of road accidents or the typicality of what happened. To consider such matters is already to decontextualize the event. Though you may come round to doing that when subsequently dealing with insurance claims or hospital bills. (Which means that you are then engaged in a *re*-contextualization of what happened.)

In the linguistic case, decontextualization / recontextualization has quite dire theoretical consequences: the sign is confused with its verbal component, and the vocal form of that component is mistaken for the sign itself. What made the utterance significant in the first place – its integration with other components of the situation – drops out of sight.

It is perhaps worth drawing attention again at this juncture to some key points in Wolf and Love's formulation of the integrationist premise. The first is that it speaks not of language or languages but of communication. Two interconnected implications should be noted.

One is that linguistic behaviour is envisaged from the start as communicational behaviour. Language is already assumed to be a mode of communication. There is consequently no way of divorcing linguistic analysis from questions of how we communicate with one another. In particular, there is no question of first describing a battery of linguistic instruments and only then inquiring how they work or what purpose they serve. (A linguistics based on this principle would presumably produce language-descriptions with the same kind of complex absurdity as the Lilliputian account of Gulliver's watch. Which, indeed, some segregationist descriptions do have. The absurdity may not strike one until one sees the description as a solemn account of the language-machine in some putative Gulliver's head.)

The second is that linguistic communication is taken to operate on the basis of signs. And signs in turn are assumed to be the *sine qua non* of all communication. So in this sense linguistics is on a par with the study of other modes of communication. It holds no privileged position. It would be fallacious, in the integrationist's view, to believe that the study of language can be divorced from the study of other forms of communication.

Here we come back to a major point of conflict with those theorists who claim or imply exactly the opposite; namely that linguistic analysis can proceed without reference at all to other forms of communicative behaviour. This is a typically segregationist view, and follows directly from treating 'the language' as an autonomous object. It is rather like claiming that chess can be described and analysed independently of any other game. (And it is no coincidence that games – including chess in particular – have often been seized on by segregational theorists as providing an analogue to languages.) But such claims are symptoms of the intellectual muddle, rather than clarifications of it. The games analogy rebounds on its proponents. For we do not have to reflect upon it very long before realizing that a description of chess (or of a particular game of chess) would be baffling unless it presupposed an understanding of what kind of activity playing is. And of 'winning', 'losing', 'game', 'opponent', etc. These are not concepts that are peculiar to chess: but chess requires a grasp of these concepts before one can make sense of it *as* a game. *Mutatis mutandis*, the same applies to language(s) and communication.

Reintegrating languages

For the integrationist, any concept of 'a language' that human beings entertain must ultimately be the product of reflection on linguistic experience, i.e. on the first-order communicational activities of speaking, listening, understanding or failing to understand, etc. It is in this sense that, in integrational linguistics, appeal to 'languages' is neither dismissed out of hand nor taken for granted, but placed on the linguist's list of explicanda. The concept of 'a language' belongs with those in terms of which individuals and communities construct a glottic identity for themselves, and in different cultures this can be done in very different ways. These ways will all in some measure rely on the reflexivity of language, but it would be naive to assume (as segregational linguistics implicitly does) that the familiar European mode of construction is basic. Rather, the European concept of 'languages', their function and their relation to communities constitutes one particular type. It is characteristic of this type to develop a metalanguage which produces formulas like 'X is the language spoken in Y' and 'X is the language spoken by the Z', where there is often a clear connexion between the name of the language (X), the name of the country (Y) and the name of the people (Z); e.g. *French, France, French*. At the other end of the scale we find language communities which do not have language-names, or where language-names do not correspond directly to ethnic designations or areas inhabited. Even in Europe, the correspondence between names for varieties of speech and names of localities is far from systematic. Thus 'He speaks broad Glaswegian' might be a way of characterizing someone's speech, but not (except humorously) 'He speaks broad Tunbridge Wellsian'.

So the integrationist answer to the question 'Do languages exist?' goes like this. If languages are supposed to be fixed codes, one of which provides the necessary basis for successful communication within every linguistic community, then their existence is an illusion. Linguistics does not need an illusion as a theoretical premise. Linguistic communication can be analysed and explained without first trying to define or redefine the language-names that happen to be in everyday use, without proposing any alternative names that might be supposed to have a more 'scientific' basis, and without supposing that there must be systems that would qualify for having such a language-name if only we could identify them. In brief, the proposition that there are languages (in the 'ontologically tough' sense) has no claim to axiomatic status in integrational linguistics.

What remains, however, is the question of languages as 'second-order' constructs. (Cf. the question of whether Christians believe that God exists versus the question of whether the God that Christians believe to exist does exist.) The word *language* is indeed a lay metalinguistic term, and as such deserves attention. No more and no less than other such terms. If in some communities linguistic communication is conceptualized and discussed in terms of 'using a language' (say, 'English'), to that extent 'the language-user already has the only concept of a language worth having' (Harris, 1980, p.3). But some people's understanding of the language-name *English* may be different from others', even though all agree that they are speakers of 'English'. For some, what underlies the language-name may be no more than a vague sense of commonality, as in an awareness of wearing the same kinds of clothes, or eating the same kinds of food. For others, what is involved may be far more specific. In the case of literate communities, the second-order construct is likely to be closely related to the forms of codification provided by grammars and dictionaries, where these exist. But it would be rash to assume that all communities have analogous metalinguistic concepts. It is also very unlikely that concepts like 'the English language' arise spontaneously from individuals' untutored reflections on their daily linguistic intercourse.

Moreover, whatever untutored reflections they do have will be influenced by the circumstances of their own linguistic community. Thus although Saussure posits the diversity of languages as a *fait primordial* it can hardly be so for any linguistic community so remote as to be unaware of the existence of communities that speak differently. 'A language' can hardly be even a second-order construct until contrasted with 'another language'. As Toolan observes, 'it is quite imaginable that speakers within a settled and isolated community might conduct themselves without ever thinking of their own speech as a language' (Toolan, 1996, p.1). The plural *languages* already assumes the state of affairs which Saussure treats as theoretically foundational. Belief in the existence of languages is just one more diagnostic of the ethnocentricity endemic in the orthodox position.

Integrational linguistics resists that ethnocentricity by treating the description of languages as description of the second-order constructs and how they are constructed. Thus instead of rushing to add to the world's stockpile of grammars and dictionaries, the integrationist will analyse the grammar of grammarians and the lexicography of lexicographers; in other words, consider grammars and dictionaries *qua* metalinguistic instruments, examine how they work, what cultural purposes they serve, what metalinguistic concepts they employ and promote. (For discussion of 'grammar' as a European cultural product, see Harris, 1987c, Ch. 5.) To the same end the integrationist will examine language-teaching programmes and their rationale (Davis, D.R., 1994). Far from being confined to merely theoretical matters, the integrationist analysis of the 'second-order construct' can have eminently practical applications of this kind.

Thus although integrationism is 'the first movement in the history of linguistics which does not attempt to extend and refine established methods and concepts of language description, or to provide them with theoretical underpinnings' (Harris, 1998b), integrationists are nevertheless very much interested in 'language description' and its influence on the way people think about language.

Language-description, however, is only one of the possible components in the construction of a glottic identity. Other metalinguistic components may involve the classification of forms of speech by reference to sex, social status, age, etc. And there may be important criteria which are recognized in the community, but are not reflected in any specific metalinguistic terminology, such as the right to speak first, the right to speak on particular occasions, at particular ceremonies, and so on.

Furthermore, the glottic identities which individuals and communities construct for themselves do not necessarily correspond to those which other individuals or other communities attribute to them. Linguistic stereotyping of various kinds and levels may feature prominently in a community's linguistic self-awareness, often with serious disadvantage resulting to particular individuals and groups. Such matters are not, for the integrationist, strictly outside the linguist's purview, a merely 'social' byproduct of linguistic behaviour, but are an intrinsic part of language.

In an integrational perspective, therefore, it would be quite unwarranted to erect a traditional European concept of languages into the main theoretical basis for analysing a mode of communication supposedly common to the whole of humanity. But this is precisely what segregational linguistics does. It is intellectually on a par with a sociology that supposes that all 'proper' societies have kings and queens (or would if they could).

It would be misconstruing the integrationist's point here to suppose that it is intended to cast doubt in any way on the validity of the lay use of language-names. 'Can you speak Spanish?' is a perfectly sensible question and can be given a perfectly sensible answer or answers. No one supposes otherwise. The issue is whether this kind of lay talk about languages justifies the linguist in making the basic assumptions about languages and their speakers that segregationists have proceeded to make.

If we are to take this question seriously, it seems necessary to examine the status of language-names a little further. Suppose that when asked if you can speak Spanish you reply that indeed you can. And suppose that your sceptical interlocutor then asks, 'But how do you know you can?' A reasonable reply for most people might run as follows: 'I know I can speak Spanish because when I go to Madrid I have no difficulty in talking to Spanish people and understanding what they say to me.' And now imagine that the sceptical interlocutor objects: 'But how do you know all these people in Madrid are speaking Spanish?' It is tempting to think that the final answer to silence this sceptic has to be: 'But that is just what speaking Spanish is, and *Spanish* is the English name of what they speak.'

The force of this kind of answer might be felt to be even greater, doubtless, if produced by a Spaniard. What, it might be asked, can possibly be objected to the claims of members of a linguistic community to know what language they are speaking? At least, provided that they all agree? The argument, in other words, is that the validation of a language-name is secured by the agreement of speakers that this indeed is the language they speak. By extension, the existence of the language is validated by its being what those speakers believe they speak. This is certainly one theoretical answer to the question 'What is a language?' that has been seriously proposed. For English, for instance, it has been claimed that 'when we take individuals collectively it is they who define what English is, and this they can do *consequent upon* believing of themselves and each other *that* they are speakers of English' (Pateman, 1983, p.120). The same argument, doubtless, could be extended to any linguistic community and any corresponding language-name.

This is worth mentioning here in order to make the point that this kind of argument will not do in order to salvage either the language myth or the segregationist position. For it begs the question at issue by presupposing the infallibility of the collectivity. It makes no difference that the beliefs of a whole group of people about themselves concur. If it did, we should presumably be obliged to accept as self-validating the proclaimed beliefs of any group about their own members' behaviour. But what credence should we attach to the claims of a sect whose members were convinced that they were reincarnations of prophets from the Old Testament? The sincerity of the beliefs is not in question either.

Many communities have doubtless in the past entertained false beliefs about themselves, and perhaps many still do. The point is that we usually require something more, against which beliefs can be measured. That is why examples of speech produced by those who claim to be speakers of English cannot be held to demonstrate evidentially the validity of that belief unless some independent criterion of what English is can be made available. The argument 'There must be an English language because we speak it' reduces upon examination to 'There must be an English language because that is what we call what we speak'. Which is far from convincing.

In practice, there is the additional snag that not all of those who claim to be speakers of a language will necessarily agree with one another about the criteria for speaking it or about one another's claims. As mentioned above, some segregationists have tried to finesse the problem by maintaining that what speakers believe about such matters is irrelevant anyway. As a reason, they adduce the claim that the commonly used language-names are in any case merely labels for vague socio-political concepts. From this it is concluded

> that any coherent account can be given of "language" in this sense is doubtful [...] Rather, all scientific approaches have simply abandoned these elements of what is called "language" in common usage. (Chomsky, 1986, p.15)

This disclaimer, however, merely declines to identify the languages hypostatized by orthodox theory with anything that speakers might believe corresponds to the commonly used language-names, or with anything that might be designated by the word 'language' on the basis of those language-names and popular beliefs associated with them. It also exemplifies the familiar segregationist ploy of identifying the segregationist position as a 'scientific approach', implying that anyone who continues to bother about investigating the 'commonsense' concept of a language is not being 'scientific'.

Nonetheless, it is noticeable that segregationists who make such disclaimers often continue to refer to, for example, 'the grammar of English', 'the sound system of English' and so on; and it is therefore legitimate to ask what these uses of the language-name *English* are supposed to imply. Hand-in-hand with this goes the question of what alternative candidate is proposed as the autonomous linguistic object, i.e. as 'the language' which the segregationist proposes to investigate.

There are two possible moves available to the segregationist here. One, already mentioned above, is to appeal to the 'idiolect', i.e. to re-locate 'the language' in the individual brain, but retain the traditional language-names as a handy way of referring collectively to groups of roughly similar languages spoken by groups of individuals. An example of this solution is provided by Smith and Wilson (1979, p.26), who maintain explicitly that 'we cannot talk of *the* grammar of English, but only of the grammars of different speakers of English'. Which is to say that 'the language' of each speaker is different. However, as Love has pointed out (Love, 1981), Smith and Wilson do not in fact follow their own advice: they proceed without further ado to talk about 'English grammar' and even describe certain types of sentence which some English speakers use as 'ungrammatical'. Love notes:

> The concept of a language which the authors feel obliged by their terms of reference to 'justify' is simply not that with which they want to work in practice. This latter turns out to be a very familiar notion, according to which English and French, for example, are languages comprising many regional, historical and personal variants, according to which it is neither false nor meaningless to say that English is a language which is often spoken ungrammatically; and so on. (Love, 1981, p.279)

But this 'very familiar notion' of a language is one which, for Smith and Wilson, has 'no systematic theoretical status at all'. Love adds:

> One consequence of this position can be illustrated as follows. The difference between your idiolect and mine is rather small. The difference between your idiolect and that of the Emperor of Japan is, doubtless, rather greater. But, according to Smith and Wilson, the difference between these differences is one of degree, not of kind. Explaining it with reference to the fact that whereas you and I speak English, the Emperor of Japan's native tongue is Japanese, simply has no place in a theoretical framework organised around the concept of a language as a set of sentences defined by the rules of an individual's grammar. (Love, 1981, p.279)

Linguistic idealizations

There is an alternative move, popular among some segregationists, which has also been mentioned in passing earlier. This involves equating 'the language' that the linguist is interested in with an 'idealization' of what is spoken in a putatively homogeneous linguistic community (Chomsky, 1980, pp.24-6). Clearly this would mean that languages, thus defined, do not exist, (as the term 'idealization' itself suggests). At first sight, it might seem that this approach is not at odds with the integrationist agnosticism about the status of 'languages'. It can be pointed out that it is no objection to say that 'real speech communities are not homogeneous' (Chomsky, 1980, p.25), since this objection ignores the fact that we are dealing with an idealization. From an integrational point of view, however, the trouble is that it is not clear that the idealization is even coherent. Love puts the problem with Chomsky's idealization as follows:

> What does it mean? In other words, how can we understand 'speech community' so as to allow for the meaningful prefixation of '(completely) homogeneous'? Or conversely, given 'homogeneous' how do we make sense of 'community'? We may wish to pose further questions. Does its homogeneity extend, for instance, to phonetic indistinguishability of tokens of the same type? Is it to be envisaged as a community in which everyone uses *exactly* the same expressions as everyone else, and means *exactly* the same things by them on all occasions of their utterance? Is it then a community in which everyone has had *exactly* the same experiences (linguistic or otherwise) as everyone else? [...] What, precisely, are we supposed to imagine that we are left with, once those aspects of the human condition which cause real speech communities to be unhomogeneous have been theoretically abstracted? (Love, 1981, p.286).

The idealization itself may be obscure, but its intended purpose is perfectly clear. It is to eliminate from consideration all forms of linguistic variation. It is to establish the fixed code as the core concept of linguistic theory and so allow the linguist to proceed on the assumption that languages are systems of fully determinate signs (i.e. determinate, in all cases, in respect of both form and meaning.) It is impossible *ex hypothesi* in such a community for one member *not* to know what linguistic signs another member is using and what they mean. It is exactly the proviso needed for Saussure's 'talking heads' model to become plausible. In such a community, no one knows any word or construction that other members do not know, or supposes that it means anything different from whatever other members suppose it to mean. Indeterminacy is thus suppressed.

Integrationism starts from exactly the opposite assumption: the human condition is such that all signs, whether linguistic or not, are intrinsically indeterminate. That assumption has profound implications for the study of language, and in particular for the study of meaning.

Further reading

- Harris and Wolf, 1998, Part 2, 'Language and the Language Myth'
- On the language myth: Harris, 1981a
- On 'standard' languages: Harris, 1987c, Ch. 5
- On 'correct' usage: Davis, H.G., 1998; Cameron, 1995

Questions for discussion

1. 'One basic difficulty is that of defining a language...It would be quite defensible if linguists would take it upon themselves to redefine the term...Unfortunately...several criteria can be proposed, no one of which is satisfactory.' (H.A. Gleason) What would be typical segregationist and integrationist ways of dealing with this difficulty?
2. 'Every human community has a language.' This has been proposed as a 'linguistic universal'. What problems would an integrationist have in accepting it?
3. 'Logically, the very notion of variation assumes knowledge of the base from which phenomena vary.' (J.B. Casagrande) For an integrationist, this stands logic on its head. Why?
4. In modern Europe we find some examples of language-names which, unlike the case of *French/France*, do not correspond to any co-named political entity. What significance would you attach to these?
5. 'Each language defines a speech community.' (C.F. Hockett) Why would an integrationist be dissatisfied with this definition?
6. Recognizable differences between *A*'s voice and *B*'s voice will often have a biomechanical basis. Why do segregationists and integrationists differ over whether such differences are linguistically irrelevant?

3

Language and Meaning

Coming across an unfamiliar word and being puzzled by it is not an unfamiliar linguistic experience. But how to interpret that experience is a controversial issue that divides linguistic theorists. To take an example at random from today's newspaper, I am puzzled by the word *moshpit*. As far as I can remember, this is the first time I have encountered it. I am tempted to ask 'What does it mean?' But there is, arguably, a prior question: 'What is it that I don't know if I don't know what it means?' This is the question that takes us into the domain of semantic theory. It is also the question that has dominated semantic theory ever since Bréal popularized the term *sémantique* in the late nineteenth century.

Meanings as concepts

The telementational view of linguistic communication, as exemplified in the Saussurean 'talking heads' model, identifies meanings as 'concepts': they are the items in the heads of A and B that in the end have to match if communication between A and B is to be successful. If the attempted conceptual matching fails, then B has not understood what A said. So on this view, looking for the meaning of *moshpit* is looking for the concept 'moshpit'. This was the concept in the journalist's brain which triggered the word *moshpit*, and my problem is that there is no corresponding concept in my brain. Or if there is, I do not recognize it as being associated with that particular linguistic form.

But this equation of meanings with concepts fell out of fashion in segregational linguistics with the rise of behaviourism. Bloomfield and his immediate followers in the USA had recourse to identifying meanings by linking linguistic forms to things in the speaker's external world (thus supposedly avoiding any 'unscientific' appeal to unobservable mental objects and processes). Furthermore, the linkage was preferably to things which 'science' had investigated and could provide a reliable account of. Bloomfield's famous paradigm example (Bloomfield, 1935, p.139) was: *salt* means 'sodium chloride (NaCl)'. He consequently had to admit that there were many words with meanings of which linguistics could give no accurate statement, since they corresponded to objects which 'science' had not yet investigated. (Among these, he admitted, were *love* and *hate*.)

This reluctance to state meanings in mentalistic terms, or in any terms that did not supposedly have backing from specialists in the physical sciences, led to a period in which linguistic semantics was allowed to languish in the doldrums. Linguists' attention switched predominantly to the description of linguistic forms. When some reference to the meanings of linguistic forms had to be made, it was made by alluding vaguely to the physical world or the speaker's 'situation'.

However, some segregationists went further than pleading absence of reliable scientific information as their excuse for neglecting semantics. It is significant, for example, that of the sixty-four chapters in a well-known textbook entitled *A Course in Modern Linguistics* published in 1958, there is not one devoted to semantics. Semantics is there said to be only a 'peripheral' linguistic subsystem. The three 'central subsystems' of any language are declared to be the grammatical system, the phonological system and the morphophonemic system; and these three are explicitly said to be central 'because they have nothing to do, directly, with the non-speech world in which speaking takes place' (Hockett, 1958, p.137). As a concise statement of segregationism, this could hardly be improved. The further from the 'non-speech world' something is, the more central it becomes for segregational linguistics.

Semantics and 'mental reality'

When behaviourism eventually fell out of favour among linguists (Chomsky, 1959), 'mentalism' came back; but came back now in an explicitly segregationist form. There was much talk of the linguist's concern with 'the mental reality' underlying verbal behaviour; but this mental reality was severely restricted in such a way as to preclude semantics from dealing with speakers' 'knowledge of the world' (Katz and Fodor, 1963). So the rehabilitation of mentalism led to no shift at all in the theoretical dividing line that segregated the linguistic from the non-linguistic, but instead to an emphatic reassertion of that division. (This was doubtless in part because at that time experimental psychologists were increasingly taking an interest in meaning, and some way had to be found of keeping linguistics safe for linguists once the behaviourist fortifications had been dismantled.)

The new picture that emerged under the aegis of generative linguistics was that of a 'native speaker' equipped with 'semantic knowledge'. The possession of this knowledge was itself part of the requirement for counting as a native speaker at all; or at least of counting as a fully competent native speaker. But what did this knowledge consist in? In the case of a native speaker of English, it appeared to consist in knowing, for example, that *bachelor* means the same as *unmarried man*, that the words *good* and *bad* are antonyms, that the sentence *Nothing white is white* is self-contradictory, that *John likes ice cream* means something different from *John collects stamps*, and indefinitely many other items of this kind. Allegedly all this, systematized in some way, constituted the sum total of the native speaker's semantic knowledge; and thus constituted *what* it was that a synchronic semantic description of that language had to describe.

The programme was certainly ambitious: indeed, if taken seriously, it meant that linguistics had hitherto failed to produce anything approaching a comprehensive semantic description of even a single language. It began to look as if the semantic project was just too vast to be manageable, even though semantic knowledge comprised only a fraction of the speaker's total knowledge. For semantic knowledge, it was repeatedly emphasized, was not to be confused with 'real world' knowledge. Thus a semantic description did not even attempt to supply the meanings that, in actual situations, speakers might take utterances to have. For in order to do that, it was argued, a semantic description of a language would need to incorporate everything about the world that members of the linguistic community happened to know; whereas the linguist's brief stopped short at explicating knowledge of 'the language'.

The first thing an integrationist would point out is that there was always an inherent puzzle in this way of delimiting segregational semantics, for it is trivially easy to match any given item of 'real world' knowledge with a corresponding putative item of 'linguistic' knowledge, given an appropriate language (Harris, 1973, pp.152-4). So it is hard to see exactly what is gained by drawing the semantic boundary in this manner. For instance, if I want to know what the unfamilar word *moshpit* means, am I not trying to find out what a moshpit is (or at least if there is such a thing?). Are not the two questions inextricably interrelated? And how can I pursue one without pursuing the other?

The metalanguage of semantics

It is not uncommon for philosophers to complain that linguists 'do not explain meaning but take it for granted. For their primitive concepts are nothing but unexplained meanings' (Devitt and Sterelny, 1987, p.102). A distinguished logician once put it bluntly, but not altogether unfairly, when he said that, pending a satisfactory explanation of the notion of meaning, 'linguists in semantic fields are in the situation of not knowing what they are talking about' (Quine, 1961, p.47). He compared the state of play in descriptive semantics to that of ancient astronomy. The astronomers observed and noted the changing positions of points of light in the night sky with commendable accuracy. But, unfortunately, they had only the most confused ideas about what these points of light actually were.

The case against segregational semantics was pressed harder still by those who condemned it as irremediably circular (Evans and McDowell 1976). It did not matter exactly how the semantic description might be formalized – whether, for instance, in terms of componential analysis or inferential rules. For – the argument ran – if the formalization merely expresses the intralinguistic semantic relations between one expression and another, then the task of explicating a native speaker's semantic knowledge has not been tackled but deferred. Thus, for instance, the part of the semantic description that formalizes the alleged synonymy relation between *bachelor* and *unmarried man* tells us nothing that was not already captured informally by saying '*bachelor* means *unmarried man*'. This merely shuffles the lexical cards that were already in the pack. What we now need to know is what *unmarried man* means. But that will involve reference to the meaning of other words: *marry*, *woman*, etc. All that has happened is that one item of postulated semantic knowledge has been related to or substituted for another, just as in a dictionary the reader is referred constantly from one entry to another or others.

This objection, it should be noted, goes one step further than Quine's complaint that linguists did not know what they were talking about. To pursue the astronomy analogy, if Evans and McDowell were right, the charge would now be that the modern lexicographer is like an ancient astronomer who is dim enough to suppose that the basic problems of astronomical investigation can be solved by drawing accurate maps of the night sky (= compiling dictionaries). But all this does is situate the positions of the points of light in relation to one another. It still does not explain what the points of light are.

Meaning and truth

What Evans and McDowell proposed was that all semantic descriptions should be stated in terms of truth conditions, in the manner first proposed by Tarski (Tarski, 1944). According to Tarski, our metalinguistic entry to semantics is provided by the fact that we can unproblematically state at least one important semantic property of a sentence like *Snow is white*, which is to state what it is for that sentence to be used to make a true statement. How do we do this? By saying: "*Snow is white*" *is true if, and only if, snow is white.* But Tarski's 'solution', as adapted by Evans and McDowell, turned out to be rather like proposing that all would be well with a map of the night sky provided the points of light were labelled so as to provide the relevant information about the universe (e.g. that this dot is the planet Venus, these dots are stars in the Pleiades, and so on).

The trouble with any such rescue package for semantics is that, once again, it postpones the problem. That is to say, if what was wrong with the uninterpreted map of the night sky was that it afforded no way of identifying a point of light except by way of its positional relation to other points of light, the trouble with the Evans-McDowell map is that all it provides in addition is a designation for each point, plus a cosmological story. But the ancients had cosmological stories too. So the improvement seems to be not in the semantics, but in the cosmology. In short, what Evans and McDowell proposed was a naively nomenclaturist solution. Designations are useful for purposes of reference, i.e. for talking about the supposed referents. But unless we understand the gloss 'This is Venus', we are none the wiser for being able to identify one point of light as 'Venus'. Behind the name there still hides a statement or statements with meaning so far unexplicated.

Semantics thus conceived is a matter of finding out what the world is 'really' like; a view which takes us back to Bloomfield's account of the meaning of *salt*. It falls under what integrationists call 'reocentric surrogationalism' (Harris, 1980, pp.44ff.) Shifting the focus of attention to truth-conditions leaves no one any the wiser about meaning. Doubtless it is comforting to receive philosophical reassurance that 'This is a moshpit' is true if and only if it *is* a moshpit. But Tarski-type semantics is the equivalent of being given a dictionary in which the entry for *moshpit* reads '*moshpit* : moshpit' (and analogously for all other entries). It also seems to be based on the curious assumption that *truth* is a more fundamental or more perspicuous metalinguistic term than *meaning*. For integrationists, 'truth' holds no privileged position in semantics.

As far as integrationists are concerned, if the snag with a semantic formula of the type '*a* means *b*' is that it is not clear what that type of formula itself means, we are no better off with one of the type '"*P*" is true if and only if *p*'. For the meaning of *that* formula is no clearer. There are still semantic unknowns: the meaning of 'true' and the meaning of *p*. Nor in the last twenty-five years has any other type of formula been proposed which does not encounter parallel objections. Orthodox semantics, whether in its linguistic or its philosophical guise, has so far failed to come up with any way out of its own semantic regress.

This, it should be noted, is *not* to say that it makes no difference for communicational purposes what a moshpit might turn out to be. It clearly does. But trying to determine the meaning of *moshpit* by establishing the truth-conditions of sentences like *This is a moshpit* makes no sense unless we have an assurance that *someone* knows what a moshpit 'really' is (i.e. knows the 'truth' about it), and that this correct view can be distinguished from views which are inadequate or mistaken. But where that assurance is supposed to come from remains quite obscure. For the integrationist, in brief, this is a programme that stands semantics on its head: for *truth* is a metalinguistic term that is presumably to be explicated by reference to the use of non-metalinguistic terms, not vice versa. In any case, when I wonder what *moshpit* means I am not looking for an ambitious account which covers any and every moshpit, i.e. identifies all and only those features common to moshpits. (For all I know, there may be no such set of features.)

Semantic determinacy

It is interesting to ask why such a bizarre programme as truth-conditional semantics was ever proposed in the first place. The integrationist answer is that the motivation can be traced directly to the fixed-code doctrine. Once it is taken for granted that the linguistic sign is a unit determinate both in form and in meaning, the inevitable search is on for some universal way of pinning down invariant, context-free meanings. These have to be meanings that are, as it were, permanently attached to vocal or written forms. They are often called 'literal' meanings, to distinguish them from 'figurative' or 'metaphorical' meanings. But the search turns out to be a wild goose chase. Why? Because there are no invariant, context-free meanings. They are the illusory abstractions conjured up by an inadequate theory of language and communication. In short, 'no such domain of context-free meaning exists' (Toolan, 1996, p.25). The segregationist is prevented from admitting this by the internal logic of the fixed code. For the fixed-code theorist, words are defined by reference to languages, *not vice versa*. Belonging to a language is what gives a word both its form and its meaning. This is the underlying assumption of segregationist semantics. Its importance cannot be overestimated. Anyone who does not grasp it will also fail to grasp the basis of integrationist semantics, which rejects this assumption.

The integrationist treats meanings not as semantic units established in advance by a fixed code, but as values which arise in context out of particular communication situations. These values are assigned by the participants as part of the integration of activities involved. It is in this sense that, for the integrationist, communication involves a constant making and re-making of meaning. It is intrinsic to the continuous creative process that our engagement with language is.

Thus assigning a meaning to *moshpit* is precisely what I have to do, somehow or other, if I want to make sense of one particular passage in a newspaper article. I could employ a number of strategies for this purpose. I could try looking up *moshpit* in a dictionary. I could ask around to find out if anyone I know is familiar with this word. Or I could make my own guess on the basis of my understanding of what else the article says.

As it happens, the word occurred in the sentence *But what the youth of Sicily do not get in the moshpit they make up for on the dance floors of Palermo's numerous discos...* The immediately preceding comment refers to the lack of pop concerts in Sicily. Which left me little the wiser. *Moshpit* = '(Sicilian) pop concert? venue for, ambiance of, (Sicilian) pop concert?' Could *pit*, I wondered, be the same *pit* as in a theatre? And therefore *mosh* a term for the audience? (?*The mosh applauded enthusiastically. ?The performance went down well with the mosh.*) But that is about as far as I could get under my own steam.

My next step was to inquire of a seasoned pop guitarist, the veteran of many 'gigs', who opined that the word was Australian. He told me that the moshpit was the area immediately in front of where the musicians played, and that moshing was the strenuous physical activity that 'sweaty fans' indulged in 'when the adrenalin was flowing' (his words) during the concert. Why it was called *moshing* he could not explain. An arbitrary sign?

With dictionaries I drew a blank, until at last Volume 3 of the *OED Additions Series* (1997) turned up trumps. There I found a hyphenated form *mosh-pit*, first attested in 1990, lurking under the lemmatic wing of a verb *mosh*, first attested in 1987, meaning 'to dance in a violent manner involving jumping up and down and deliberately hitting other dancers, esp. at a rock concert'. I noted the implication of aggression, that my guitarist informant had not hinted at. The verb *mosh* was said to be 'slang' of US origin, perhaps etymologically connected with the verbs *mash* or *mush*. (These latter suggestions seemed to be offered without a great deal of lexicographical conviction.)

Here we already have a number of problems for orthodox linguistics (such as how and when exactly a word gains admission to 'the English language' and who admits it) which we will ignore for the moment in order to focus on more fundamental issues.

The trivial example of my first encounter with *moshpit* is one which, when viewed in an integrationist perspective, illustrates a number of quite basic points about meaning. 1. All words begin, in our experience, as words of 'unknown meaning'. There is no genetically programmed dictionary in the brain in which to 'look them up'. If there were, parents would be deprived of one of their main linguistic functions, and we should have no use for overt questions like 'What does this word mean?' 2. 'Meaning' is the value we seek to attribute to words so as to make some kind of sense of this or that episode of communication in which they feature. 3. Our search for the 'meaning' stops when we have discovered how to integrate the occurrence of the word into enough of our linguistic experience to satisfy the requirements of the case. 4. This will suffice, provided we do not come across further cases which seem to require a different or more elaborate explanation. (Whether this will happen in the *moshpit* case I do not know, since I have come across no further cases than those reported above.) 5. Our search for the 'meaning' is articulated to a large extent metalinguistically (by asking questions, consulting dictionaries, etc.), i.e. is essentially dependent on the reflexivity of language. Without that, what would I have done? Gone off to Sicily and hung out around the discos hoping for enlightenment? Life is too short to bother about such matters. For most of us 'meaning is always "now"' (Toolan, 1990, p.154).

The great mistake the orthodox semanticist makes is not being content with this humble wisdom, but insisting that *moshpit* (if it is a genuine word) must have a 'real' (= determinate) meaning known at least to those ideal speakers of whatever language (= fixed code) it belongs to.

A further, consequential mistake would be supposing that coming across a word for the first time is a 'special case' and therefore unreliable as a guide to 'the nature of meaning'. The integrationist, on the contrary, maintains that what happens in this 'special case' is what happens in *every* case, except that the similarity is disguised by our hubristic readiness to assume that our past linguistic experience provides all the information we need in order to assign semantic values in present and future cases.

It should be noted that even now I know very little about how those people familiar with the word *mosh-pit* use it. I do not know, for instance, whether or not it is regarded as a derogatory term (which would possibly be relevant if I wanted to use it in future conversations). I do not know what alternative designations, if any, are available in the vocabulary of those who frequent pop concerts. I do not know whether the area of the moshpit is bounded or flexible, depending on the amount of moshing going on at any particular concert. And so on. But at present I have no particular interest in pursuing these questions. Why not? Because I have already discovered enough for my immediate communicational needs. I can give it a meaning which makes sense of what I read in the paper.

Meanings and intentions

So far, however, no mention has been made of the other actor in the original semantic drama; namely, the journalist in whose article the word *moshpit* occurred. Does the author have no say in what the word means? How do I know that what the author thought it meant corresponds to what the *OED* lexicographers say it means? Or does it mean that *in spite of* whatever my author thought? Was I, as a potential holiday-maker, being obliquely warned by the use of the word *moshpit* not to venture into Sicilian discos, because the dancing was particularly aggressive, expressive of *machismo*, etc.? Or did the author of the article have no such intention?

Here we come to the alternative explanation of meaning which has proved most popular among those sceptical about a truth-conditional account; namely, the explanation which bases meaning on speaker's intentions (Grice, 1957; Strawson, 1970). The intentional account derives a great deal of its immediate plausibility from the fact that we commonly use the word *mean* to express intention (*I meant to do it, but I forgot*), plus the fact that most of our speech is indeed intended to acquaint others with our views, hopes, fears, wishes, etc. Hence, looking for the meaning of a word is easily assimilated to trying to fathom the intentions of its user(s).

Humpty Dumpty is perhaps the most famous champion of the thesis that words mean whatever the speaker wants them to. His argument with Alice about the meaning of the word *glory* has become a kind of symbolic anecdote in modern semantic theory. Humpty Dumpty's thesis, patently, is quite unacceptable to the fixed-code theorist. In fixed-code semantics, it is the code that determines the meaning, not the speaker. And yet it seems undeniable that people do often ask others what they mean in order to clarify a remark; and undeniable that this is often a sensible strategy. If I had been able to ask the author of the article what *moshpit* meant, presumably that would have settled the question to my satisfaction. (It would, at any rate, have been disconcerting to get the reply 'I don't know'. People are expected to take linguistic responsibility for the words they use, at least to the extent of being able to explain what they mean if called upon to do so.)

Yet none of this makes integrationists enthusiastic about joining the ranks of those who propound intentionalist theories of meaning. One reason for this is that putting the speaker in charge of meaning seems tantamount to denying that the hearer has any role to play at all, other than a purely passive one. Another reason is that it is far from clear that the appeal to speaker's intentions is in the end any more than the beginning of another semantic regress. For it seems extremely difficult to disengage the 'intention' from the actual words used to express it. (*A*'s intention in saying '*p*' was to express – and to be understood as expressing – the idea that *p*. This takes us nowhere, except back to the problem of 'mentalese'. Or perhaps to the notion that what *A* can intend to say is determined by what *A*'s language allows to be said. Which is back to a version of the fixed code.) Just as in truth-conditional semantics, the theoretical boot seems somehow to have been put on the wrong foot. In everyday communication, we generally assess people's intentions by what they say; not what they say by their intentions.

Stipulative definition

Modern semantic theory has thus steered an uncertain course between the shallows of intention and the rocky reef of truth. One begins to see why utopian linguistics so desperately needs its ideal speaker-hearers and its homogeneous communities. For wherever we look in 'real life' we seem to find only an unfathomed expanse of semantic doubt, in which the half-blind lead the blind (i.e. those with *any* claim to know lead those with a less impressive – or no such – claim).

The integrationist's rejection of Humpty-Dumptyism should not be construed as a refusal to accept that a word can be made to mean what its sponsor wants it to mean. What Humpty Dumpty was doing is sometimes called 'stipulative definition'. What the integrationist will say is that if stipulative definition is not to cause more problems than it solves, careful attention must be paid to the integrational requirements of the situation. An actual case history will illustrate the point. The Humpty Dumpty in this instance is the distinguished biologist Richard Dawkins, who invented the word *meme*. That Dawkins clearly recognizes the integrational requirements is evident from the passage in which he introduces his new coinage.

> We need a name for the new replicator, a noun which conveys the idea of a unit of cultural transmission, or a unit of *imitation*. 'Mimeme' comes from a suitable Greek root, but I want a monosyllable that sounds a bit like 'gene'. I hope my classicist friends will forgive me if I abbreviate mimeme to *meme*. If it is any consolation, it could alternatively be thought of as being related to 'memory', or to the French word *même*. It should be pronounced to rhyme with 'cream'. (Dawkins, 1976, p.206)

He then goes on to give examples of the kind of thing a meme is: 'tunes, ideas, catch-phrases, clothes fashions, ways of making pots or of building arches'. And an account of the typical 'behaviour' of memes:

> Just as genes propagate themselves in the gene pool by leaping from body to body via sperms or eggs, so memes propagate themselves in the meme pool by leaping from brain to brain via a process which, in the broad sense, can be called imitation. (Dawkins, 1976, p.206)

It is interesting that Dawkins does not appear to notice that the whole of language constitutes part of humanity's meme pool, if we are to take this account at face value. But the more important point for our present purposes is that, unlike Humpty Dumpty, Dawkins takes no perverse delight in withholding semantic information. (Alice would have found him a far more congenial conversationalist than Carroll's perverse egg.) Dawkins clearly wants his *meme* to be a meme itself. (Reflexivity once more.) And to this end he takes great care that we understand (i) how to integrate this unfamilar term into future episodes of discourse, and (ii) how we are to regard it as fitting in to integrational patterns with which we may already be familiar. Hence his concern to choose a form which can be seen as related to the Greek *mimesis*, the French *même*, the English *memory*. These are all links of lexical 'motivation' (to use Saussure's term), but they are integrational links as well.

It is also interesting to note that Dawkins' careful coinage has already been accepted as an English word by the *OED* lexicographers (although they give it a definition which, arguably, does less than justice to Dawkins' original idea). But what all this shows fairly convincingly is that the fixed code is a quite inadequate model if we wish to understand the processes by which verbal meanings are made. Where was the public semantic code that assigned *meme* its meaning? (It could hardly have been hidden away in the recesses of Dawkins' brain.) Words have no meanings other than those which they are given as tools for the articulation of discourse. This Dawkins clearly understands and takes advantage of for his own purposes. There is no obligation on anyone to 'accept' the word *meme*, or to use it, whether in accordance with Dawkins' intentions or in any other way: and there is quite a good case for rejecting it outright, on the ground that Dawkins' whole analogy with genes is a piece of confused thinking from beginning to end.

Demythologizing semantics

Taking an integrational approach to meaning involves seeing that some of the classic problems of orthodox semantics are not so much to be resolved as to be dismissed.

An illustrative example is provided by the old chestnut of 'homonymy' and 'polysemy'. This arises in synchronic linguistics because a comprehensive description of the fixed code requires the linguist to identify a determinate number of forms and allocate to each a determinate meaning or meanings. The problem was set up in canonical fashion by Bloomfield when he pointed out the difficulty of deciding whether what he called 'the English verb *bear*' in, for example, *bear a burden, bear troubles, bear fruit* and *bear offspring* is to be regarded as 'a single form' or as a set of 'two or perhaps even more homonyms' (Bloomfield, 1935, p.145).

This is a debate that has dragged on among linguists for many years. Both polysemy and homonymy are, according to the orthodox analysis, aspects of the phenomenon usually known as 'multiple meaning'. In cases of multiple meaning, two or more meanings are associated with a single form. (Note the underlying assumption that the language code is a simple bi-planar structure.) The difference between cases of polysemy and cases of homonymy is alleged to be that in polysemy we have several distinct meanings of a single word, whereas in homonymy we have two or more words, which simply happen to coincide in form.

There are countless puzzles of this type. Are there two English words *nail*, one of which designates a metal spike and the other a growth of horn at the tip of the finger? Or is there just one word *nail*, which has these two meanings? Are there two words *cob*, one for a type of hazelnut and the other for a type of horse? Or is there just one word with two quite different meanings? Examples could be multiplied *ad nauseam*.

The traditional way of dealing with such cases lexicographically often appealed to two factors. One was etymology. Thus if the form in question was known to have had two quite different sources, the dictionary would list them as two separate words. For this reason, in most English dictionaries at least three nouns *bank* are recorded. One *bank* means 'a raised shelf of ground', another *bank* means 'an institution engaged in lending and borrowing money' and the third *bank* means a 'bench or tier'. They count as different words because they have different linguistic histories. One 'comes from' Germanic, one from Old Norse and one from French or Italian.

The snag here for synchronic linguistics is that the lexicographical solution appeals to historical factors and this is inadmissible evidence for the descriptive linguist. So some other way has to be found of settling the issue.

The other traditional criterion applied by lexicographers was that of spelling. Thus in English dictionaries *flower* is listed as a separate word from *flour*, even though they are said to derive etymologically from the same source. This criterion too is inadmissible in orthodox linguistics, as a consequence of the fact that writing is treated as constituting a different form of communication (see Ch. 5). The language is the spoken language and sound is its medium, not paper and ink. So again some other way round the difficulty has to be found.

In any case, as the above examples illustrate, the criteria of etymology and orthography often conflict, so they would not be much help to the linguist anyway. What the linguist needs in order to distinguish between homonymy and polysemy is a single criterion, or an internally consistent set of criteria, which can be applied in all cases and will yield an unequivocal result. Unfortunately, the requirement is difficult to satisfy because the 'evidence' in many instances is ambivalent.

For example, Ullmann (1959, p.115) discusses the case of the Italian form *capo*, which in some areas of Northern Italy turns up not only with the meaning 'head' but also with the meaning 'wheel hub'. At first sight this might appear to be a case of homonymy. But, according to Ullmann, this is not so, as is shown by the fact that in a number of adjacent areas *capo* with the meaning 'wheel hub' has been replaced by *testa*, and *testa* also means 'head'. This proves, claims Ullmann, that the two meanings of *capo* have been 'apprehended as two senses of the same word and not as two separate words, i.e. as polysemantic and not as homonymous'.

The case is interesting because it highlights all kinds of difficulties in the rationale of orthodox semantics. In the first place, the argument Ullmann gives is not strictly admissible in court, because it cites both evidence from linguistic change (the replacement of *capo* by *testa*) and also evidence from neighbouring dialects. But each dialect, considered from an orthodox synchronic point of view, is an independent system, an autonomous object. The linguist cannot appeal to evidence from one dialect in order to analyse another, any more than evidence from Chinese can be used in the analysis of English. That the dialects happen in this instance to be geographical neighbours is, strictly speaking, an irrelevance.

In the second place, it is crucial to the example to observe what question Ullmann is asking. He is trying to ascertain whether this is a case of homonymy or polysemy *for the speakers themselves.* In other words he is trying to investigate the 'psychological reality' of the situation. The simplest hocus-pocus solution would be for the linguist to take an arbitrary decision to classify all identical forms as belonging to the same word, irrespective of any differences in meaning. The objection to that, from a Saussurean or God's-truth point of view, is that such a description fails to capture the psychological reality. In other words, the claim is that differences of meaning *do* matter when it comes to whether speakers of the language recognize one word or more than one word in any given set of cases.

Ullmann's treatment of his Italian example is interesting because it falls between the two stools. He claims to be looking for the description that corresponds to the psychological reality of the case; but in fact supplies a hocus-pocus argument. In other words, his appeal to what happens in neighbouring dialects is a tacit appeal to consistency of description. The implied reasoning presupposes that the linguist will want to be able to exhibit parallel descriptions for analogous states of affairs. Whereas in theory what the linguist should be seeking to establish is how matters stand for each particular linguistic community. And it is not beyond the bounds of possibility that two neighbouring communities would react differently to similar linguistic situations, just as they might react differently to similar political or religious situations. The weakness in Ullmann's argument is precisely that in some dialects *testa* has replaced *capo* as a designation for the wheel hub, whereas in other dialects it has not. Ullmann cites this as evidence for his preferred solution, whereas it is arguably evidence against it.

Here we see the iceberg tip of the more general problem for orthodox linguistics. What exactly do linguistic descriptions describe? The answer that they describe – or should describe – the linguistic facts is at best a tautology and at worst an evasion of the issue. For the question then recurs in the form 'What is a linguistic fact?' (see Ch. 6). The integrationist will point out that orthodox linguistics has never provided a satisfactory answer to this question; and will argue furthermore that no satisfactory answer is available within the straitjacket imposed by the fixed-code doctrine.

Integrational semantics

Integrational semantics starts from the assumption that there are no autonomous signs or systems of signs: which in turn entails that formal and semantic determinacy are not basic properties of signs, *either in language or in any other mode of communication.* So there is no answer to the decontextualized question of what *moshpit* 'really' means, or whether *capo* 'really' is one word or two.

Critics of integrationism sometimes regard this assumption as paradoxical, since they see it as implying that all attempts by humans to understand one another are doomed to failure. But it is the postulate of determinacy which leads to paradox, at least in linguistics. Here we see how the reflexivity of language resists any attempt by linguists to suspend it for their own professional convenience. It is because the formulas of descriptive semantics are themselves semantically problematic that they must ultimately fail in the attempt to assign determinate meanings to the linguistic expressions they purport to identify. What is being attempted in segregational semantics is both a theoretical and a practical impossibility; but above all a *linguistic* impossibility.

To say this, it should be noted, is not to dismiss as nonsensical such statements as '*bachelor* means *unmarried man*', or '*moshpit* means *area in front of the musicians*'. What is at issue is not whether such statements might make sense, but whether their role is that which is claimed for them in orthodox linguistics. According to the integrationist, the claim was mistaken from the start. Can an alternative account of such statements be given? The integrationist answer is that it not only can be but must be given if we are fully to grasp what kind of mistake was made in the first place and avoid making it again.

The integrationist alternative runs, in brief, as follows. Statements of the type '*a* means *b*' (where *a* and *b* are both linguistic expressions) cannot be regarded *a priori* as statements about anyone's semantic knowledge. But they can be regarded as making sense – in those circumstances where they *do* make sense – as statements by participants engaged in a certain type of metalinguistic practice. This will typically involve giving an answer of the general form '*a* means *b*' on occasions where, for some reason, the question 'What does *a* mean?' arises. This pattern is evidence of what may be called a **'glossing**

practice'. Such a practice is what I am engaged in when I ask my guitarist 'What does *moshpit* mean?' and get the answer 'It means the area immediately in front of where the musicians play'.

The study of glossing practices in different linguistic communities and different types of situation is, for the integrationist, an important part of semantics. Glossing practices, both within and between linguistic communities, are among the familiar resources available for reducing semantic indeterminacy.

What is missing from orthodox semantics is any serious attempt to elucidate glossing practices. That failure is the result of a series of nested mistakes. It is as if an economic theorist had made the error of supposing that all you need to know about the economic system is how to write a cheque and cash one. The integrationist objection is that unless you know what you can do with the cash, you have *still* not grasped anything that could be called an economic fact. Economic facts do not exist in a self-contained economic vacuum. They are integrated products of many different activities. So too are linguistic facts.

The point is that knowing how to write and cash a cheque may indeed be part of everyday economic competence in some societies; but theorists who fail to realize that these are only second- or third-order processes which themselves require explication in more basic economic terms are failing to address the problem. The failure would be tantamount to proceeding as if what went on in banks bore no relation to anything going on elsewhere, but constituted a self-contained world of its own.

Semantics and literacy

Part of the problem is a failure to realize to what extent orthodox linguistics is the linguistics of Western literacy. Familiarity with the dictionary has warped perceptions of what is required of semantic theory. The dictionary is not a magical, self-explanatory text. Nor is it a compendium of the community's semantic knowledge. It is doubtful whether it is even a compendium of the community's glossing practices, even though it offers a conspicuous example of one such type of practice.

And it is with these practices that the linguist must begin if any progress is to be made beyond the dead end into which segregational semantics has diverted the study of linguistic meaning. What is remarkable is how little effort linguists have devoted to analysing the glossing practices that have become commonplace in literate communities. We buy and consult dictionaries. But no one examines the use we make of them, what store we set by them, or how or to what extent they are invoked to resolve disagreements about meaning. The linguist gets cold feet here, and tends to complain that these are inquiries for sociologists or educationists. (Or for any other academic specialists you can think of, provided linguists are excused.) What is true of dictionaries is true of other glossing practices, in both literate and pre-literate communities. The notion that such studies should be taken seriously is the starting point for an integrational semantics.

But it means getting away from the assumption that the teacher who tells you, for instance, 'Ice floats in water' thereby implements or invokes a certain semantic structure which 'the English sentence *Ice floats in water*' already possessed or represented, including the meanings of the individual words or morphemes of which it is composed. It is precisely this kind of assumption that seems to be given powerful support by the information provided in ordinary monolingual dictionaries. There the lexicographer has set out the meanings of individual words of the language in question. The meanings of these words are presented as being independent of their use by any particular speaker or writer. The meaning belongs to the word, not to the user. So, for example, the word *ice* is deemed to have a specific meaning or set of meanings, which users can discover by looking the word up in *Webster's* or the *Oxford English Dictionary*; and when they use this word in discourse they are deemed to have implemented or invoked or appealed to this meaning (or one of the specified meanings of the word if more than one is given). According to the segregationist, that is what *must* happen, for at least two reasons. One is that those who nowadays use the word *ice* did not invent it; it was already there in 'the English language' before they were born. Secondly, individuals just do not have the power to change the established meanings of words, even if they wanted to. So on both counts the segregational approach to meaning seems to square with common sense; and that is part of its powerful appeal.

What supposedly happens when the speaker says e.g. 'Ice floats in water' is that any hearer who speaks the same language is able to recognize this form of words, to grasp that what has been uttered is a sentence of that language and to understand what it means, i.e. to comprehend both its grammatical structure and its semantics.

This basic fixed-code account can be embroidered in various ways. But as an account of meaning and communication it has various attractions which it would be foolish to underestimate. 1. It is an extremely simple account, and this in itself is a bonus. The integrationist cannot match it for simplicity and is forced to tell a much more complicated story. 2. The account immediately yields an explanation of communication. In order to understand how *A* communicates to *B* the information that ice floats in water, all that needs to be postulated is that both *A* and *B* have access to the same fixed code in which *Ice floats in water* is included among the grammatical sentences. 3. The account is one which, at least on first inspection, appears not only to be internally coherent but also to correspond to what happens in 'real life'. In other words, we seem to be born into a world in which a language is already in place: a language in which the word *ice* means 'ice', the word *water* means 'water', and so on. Furthermore, although we may learn other languages than our first language, those languages too are always there in advance of our learning them. So the view that they have an autonomous existence does not clash with our language-learning experience. 4. The account is able to circumvent any difficulties that might arise from variations in the circumstances under which signs are used from one occasion to the next, including variation in the participants. For if the code is fixed, then by definition it remains unaffected by changes of circumstance. *Ice floats in water* means the same, whether uttered by a bishop to an actress, or an actress to a bishop, and whether in Tottenham or in Timbuktu. (Chess remains chess, whether the game is played in Moscow or New York, by princes or paupers, with pieces of ivory or of plastic.) 5. Finally, the account can be presented as not merely one that corresponds to observable facts but, perhaps more impressively still, as one that in some sense *must* be right. For is it not a logical requirement that linguistic rules, like the rules of chess, must already be in place before there can be any question of individuals following or conforming to them?

Given these advantages, it is hardly surprising that the fixed-code approach to semantics found favour with so many twentieth-century theorists, even though they might differ profoundly on other linguistic matters.

Fixed-code semantics, however, has its problems. Some of these have already been illustrated above with the *moshpit* and *meme* examples. When we come across words we do not know, words which apparently did not exist a few years ago, it is difficult to resist two conclusions. One is that if there are verbal 'codes', they cannot be fixed: on the contrary, they must be changing all the time. The other conclusion is that if there are such codes, different people use different ones, and these too change. Until yesterday, mine did not include the word *moshpit*: today it does.

But if the code has the kind of instability evidenced by the sudden emergence of new words and meanings, what guarantee of stability is there for 'old' words and meanings? The integrationist sees none. And if indeed there is none, then it is the viability of the concept of the code that is itself called in question. For it conspicuously fails to fulfil the theoretical function that is required of a code in semantics; namely, to provide a source for those publicly invariant meanings that supposedly underpin verbal communication in the community, and can consequently be both 'encoded' and 'decoded' by those who know the code.

Shoring up the fixed code

Theorists who have spotted the problem have often supposed that the answer is to shore up the fixed code. They conceded that postulating a fixed code known to both *A* and *B* is not *sufficient* to explain everything there is to be explained about how *B* actually interprets *A*'s message. For, they agree, *B* may know many things that will or could affect that interpretation, and these other things have nothing to do with the code as such (knowing, for instance, who *A* is, knowing that *A* already knows many things about *B*, knowing what they have previously agreed, etc.) From this general observation springs the notion that in assessing what *A* means, *B* needs to supplement the semantic knowledge, used in decoding the verbal signs, with various other kinds of information. The study of various facets of this supplementation is variously said to be the province of 'pragmatics' or of 'paralinguistics' or of 'speech act theory' or of 'relevance theory' or of 'text linguistics', etc., depending on the particular interests and academic orientation of the proponents. Accordingly distinctions are drawn between 'sentence meaning', 'utterance meaning', 'speaker's meaning' and so on, in order not to confuse the semantic contribution that supposedly comes from knowing the code with the contribution that supposedly comes from external sources. All of this is part and parcel of what one might call the 'fixed-code-plus' account of meaning.

An integrationist will certainly agree that *B* needs to know more than the dictionary meanings of the words *A* utters in order to understand what *A* is saying, but will point out that if any of the 'extra' things *B* needs to know are construed as being just extra to *B*'s semantic knowledge, then (i) the fixed-code theory is still in place, and (ii) this additional knowledge required for successful communication is already being defined in a question-begging way (i.e. as something 'extra' to a body of knowledge that has never been satisfactorily established in the first place). It is tantamount to building an extra storey on to a theoretical structure that is already founded on sand.

'Fixed-code-plus' semantics produces an account of communication which is impressive only if we fail to notice that it starts from assumptions that already anticipate its conclusions. Its internal coherence is the coherence of circularity. Its apparent correspondence with our day-to-day linguistic experience is based on selecting questions that do indeed arise in everyday circumstances, *but then decontextualizing these questions.*

For example, questions of the form: 'What is the meaning of the word *x*?' This is a perfectly reasonable kind of question to ask when someone comes across an unfamiliar word. But it is a puzzling question when asked in connexion with a word that is not at all unfamiliar. Compare 'What is the meaning of the word *entropy*?' with 'What is the meaning of the word *house*?'. The latter might be a question asked by Pierre learning English, but hardly by Peter who has been speaking English all his life, *unless in connexion with some particular context of occurrence.* (Such a context might be the provisions of a will or other legal document. But ruminations on the meaning-in-general of the English word-in-general *house* must be counted as belonging to the self-inflicted occupational hazards of the lexicographer or the linguistic philosopher.)

However, once the general, decontextualized question is allowed to slip by as the model for a valid form of theoretical inquiry (i.e. one for which an answer must be provided in respect of each and every item in the linguistic lexicon) the way is already paved for the fixed-code answer. There is, indeed, no other available answer. By selecting such questions in advance as key questions, the discourse of 'fixed-code-plus' semantics seeks insurance against any possibility of subversion.

At the same time, this discourse invariably casts each individual in the role of the *user* of signs, a role which already implies that there is something available to be used, i.e. the signs themselves. Thus *ab initio* what the individual can do in the communicational process is severely restricted. Freedom of manœuvre is limited to choosing how to utilize a stock of verbal resources all provided in advance. This division between what the individual can and cannot do is precisely the division given canonical status in the Saussurean distinction between *parole* and *langue*. All that needs to be added is an account of *what else* the interlocutors A and B need to know in order to communicate.

Making meaning

The integrational alternative to this kind of discourse is based on the premise that human beings are not mere language-users: they are language-makers. The integrational perspective sees us as making linguistic signs as we go; and as having no alternative but to do this, because language is time-bound. For the integrationist, we are time-bound agents, in language as in all other activities. There is no way we can step outside the time-track of communication. Once this is conceded, it follows that there is no such thing as a contextless sign. A sign cannot exist except in some temporally circumscribed context. That contextualization is a foundational condition of the very existence of the sign. And that is why there is no question of giving any *general* account of 'what else' A and B need to know, apart from their fixed code.

In short, we are brought to recognize what the integrationist calls the **'principle of cotemporality'**. The chronological integration of language with events in our daily lives requires us to suppose that what is said is immediately relevant to the current situation, unless there is reason to suppose otherwise. But this applies not only to what we say but to everything we do. In other words, in this respect there is a complete parity of status between linguistic acts and other acts. Linguistic acts do not have some special temporal status of their own, which somehow puts them outside the sequentiality of the rest of our existence. This might be thought to be an extremely banal observation, and in one sense it is. But it is perhaps worth calling a 'principle' when we realize how far-reaching its implications are for linguistic inquiry.

The way the principle of cotemporality impinges on semantics is as follows. It obliges the linguist to recognize that language does not provide us with a miraculous guarantee of the stability of meaning(s) over time, or even from one moment to the next. To demand such a guarantee for any mode of communication is to demand an impossibility.

The general point may be illustrated by a very simple example:

> *A* says: 'It looks like rain.'
> *B* says: 'What did you say?'
> *A* says: 'It looks like rain.'

This appears on first inspection to be a paradigm case of what people call 'repetition', and one of the things commonly assumed about speech is that anything that is said can always be repeated. Such an assumption is indeed taken for granted in segregationist discussions of language: all that is required is a simple reiteration of the words previously uttered.

However, if the principle of cotemporality is observed, i.e. if the integrationist is right in claiming that speech communication can only take place where and when it does on any given occasion (i.e. subject to certain biomechanical, macrosocial and circumstantial conditions), then construal of repetition as merely 'doing the same thing over again' immediately becomes problematic. And this is confirmed when we reflect that in *A*'s second utterance in the above exchange *A* does *not* say the same thing as in the first utterance, even though 'the same words' (in one similarly problematic sense) may be said to be spoken. Uttering 'the same words' is neither a necessary nor a sufficient condition for 'saying the same thing'.

Now this is exactly what the principle of cotemporality predicts, because the contextualization of *A*'s second utterance is irreducibly different from that of the first. *A*'s second utterance is a reply to the question 'What did you say?', whereas the first is not. The second utterance may be construed as a quotation of the first; whereas the first utterance can hardly be construed as a quotation of the second. The answer 'What I said was that it looks like rain', which would be a perfectly reasonable reply to *B*'s question, cannot stand as a paraphrase of the first utterance.

All these considerations point to the error in the simplistic concept of linguistic repetition as 'saying the same thing over again'. Saying the same thing over again is no more a theoretical possibility in language than scoring the same goal over again is a theoretical possibility in football. A second goal is another goal, regardless of who scores it or how.

It would be obtuse to object to this on the ground that the sense in which A 'says the same thing' is just the sense in which the same sentence is uttered twice. For that would be like arguing that the second goal was simply the first goal scored again. Now there may indeed be similarities in the ways the two goals were scored, as there may be between A's first and second utterances: but the point in contention between the segregationist and the integrationist concerns the status of this invariant abstraction – 'the sentence'.

When we describe someone as having repeated what he or she said previously, we are doing no more than characterize a later act by reference to some contextually pertinent features of an earlier act, just as when we say of the postman that he knocked on the door twice. One knock was followed by a second knock. How much further we can pin down the 'sameness' then depends on the linguistic resources available, plus whatever communicational strategies can be recruited from mimicry or recording. (Perhaps the second knock was louder than the first, or more muffled, or coincided with the baby crying, etc. The differences, however pronounced, do not invalidate the 'sameness' already presupposed by saying that the postman knocked *twice*.) What is important is to see that *twice* has no meaning except in virtue of invoking a chronological scenario. Sameness itself is time-bound. Which is another way of formulating the principle of cotemporality.

The problematic and contingent character of the samenesses involved in repeating what is said becomes evident as soon as we reflect on the possibility that A's second utterance in the hypothetical exchange instanced above might have been something else: e.g. 'Rain is forecast'. Does this count as repetition or not? The answer is far from clear. Far from clear, that is, unless we know a great deal more about the communication situation. Much more than is recoverable from the isolated report of the exchange. (Are A and B standing side by side looking up at the sky? Is A commenting on the weather report in a newspaper that B has not yet read? What were the immediately preceding remarks?)

In short, instances of repetition do not provide counterexamples to the principle of cotemporality: on the contrary, they confirm it. Nor do they show that, in some cases at least, communication depends on the existence of invariant signs. Again, on the contrary, what they show is the dependence of 'repetition' on the circumstances of communication.

Semantic indeterminacy

A second way in which the principle of cotemporality projects a distinctively integrational approach to meaning lies in the acknowledgement of semantic indeterminacy in all forms of human communication. More exactly, the integrational claim is that 'insofar as what is meant is determinate, it can only be a provisional determinacy, relativized to a particular interactional situation' (Harris, 1981a, p.167). The key phrase here is the oxymoron *provisional determinacy*. If the determinacy is only provisional, then it is no more to be relied on than honour among thieves

Why does cotemporality entail semantic indeterminacy? Because to say that communication is intrinsically time-bound is to say that all assignments of meaning are made by time-bound agents. We have no alternative but to interpret particular episodes of communication by integrating them into the unique temporal sequence of events which constitutes our previous experience. Which in turn entails that where two or more participants are involved a message must be open to two or more interpretations. And these cannot be guaranteed to coincide. Furthermore, where they conflict, no one interpretation holds a privileged position *vis-à-vis* another.

Now a world in which semantic indeterminacy was acknowledged as an insoluble *obstacle* to communication would be a deeply disturbing world for most people to live in. It would in effect condemn each of us to living in perpetual solitary confinement – a view of the human condition which some great writers have, paradoxically, presented in their most widely acclaimed works. But in addition to the fact that we do not like feeling isolated, there is also the fact that we like to feel we live in a stable communicational environment. And both these requirements are in various ways threatened by semantic indeterminacy.

That is why human beings have developed two basic strategies for dealing with semantic indeterminacy. One is the simple strategy of ignoring it wherever possible. The other is the more complex strategy of trying to devise means of limiting or circumscribing its consequences. These efforts at circumscription result in many diverse cultural institutions, from calendars and legislative codes to dictionaries. All these are semantic instruments. And from an integrational point of view, semantics might be broadly defined as **the study of the limitation of semantic indeterminacy in human affairs**. Doubtless for many purposes, linguistic and other, life would be simpler if there were no indeterminacy. But confusing desiderata with reality is not the best basis on which to erect a theoretically sound semantics. In any case, the integrationist must not be taken to assume that limiting semantic indeterminacy is somehow a desirable goal in itself, or one implicitly presupposed in all forms of communication. In many cases semantic indeterminacy of a certain kind or at a certain level is actually sought.

Vague answers are useful when we do not wish to commit ourselves. We all know the wily politician whose public discourse as a whole might be seen as a constant exercise in keeping options open while at the same time appearing to give assurances. Poetry and other forms of imaginative literature would be the poorer if deprived of the scope for hinting, suggesting, alluding. Humour would be hamstrung if language afforded no possibility of ambiguity.

Integrational semantics recognizes all this, while rejecting the assumption that words have meanings, at least in the sense in which that is maintained by segregational theorists. That is to say, for the integrationist meanings are not fixed semantic values which somehow attach to particular verbal (or other) forms *irrespective of the communicational circumstances*. According to the integrationist, to believe in invariant semantic values is to subscribe to the same kind of myth as the idea that the pound sterling is a monetary unit worth a guaranteed amount. (This is the economic myth that leads naive people to 'save' by hoarding coins and notes in boxes under the bed.) As in the case of money, value is not established *a priori*, but is what human beings create as the product of significant activity.

The semantics of lexicography

One immediate consequence of the integrational approach to meaning is a quite different view of lexicography from that adopted by orthodox linguists. At first sight, the very existence of the cultural institution we call the dictionary might appear to provide irrefutable evidence in favour of orthodox semantics. The monolingual dictionary, after all, appears to set out the words we use, along with their meanings: both words and meanings being presented as decontextualized abstractions. How would this be possible if words had no such meanings? Or if their being meaningful at all depended on their users and the precise circumstances of their use?

The integrationist takes a radically different view of the dictionary. From an integrational perspective, a dictionary appears as one of the institutions developed in literate societies to promote attempts to limit semantic indeterminacy. Furthermore, the integrationist sees a dictionary as an essentially communicational enterprise, which cannot get off the ground at all without the lexicographer making certain communicational assumptions; namely, assumptions about why readers may wish to consult the dictionary. Depending on what those assumptions are, the dictionary entries will be appropriate or inappropriate. But the correlation comprising 'lemma plus gloss' is not to be read as the formulation of one specific semantic truth *about the language*. It does not set out an array of fixed values which are invariant under the operation of lexical substitution – or any other operation for that matter.

What happens in a dictionary, according to the integrational account, is that the lexicographer *proposes* correlations, as distinct from *reporting* them. In a given tradition of lexicography, this will often take the form of either endorsing or failing to endorse the proposals of previous lexicographers; but this does not alter the basic nature of the enterprise. Nor is it altered by the fact that lexicographers may often claim a somewhat different status for their endeavours.

For the integrationist, the lexicographer – like everyone else – is a language-maker; but one whose professional language-making is constrained by a particular type of glossing practice: the lexical entry which states the meaning of one word in terms of another word or words. The paradox is that the formula the lexicographer uses in order to systematize semantic information is itself semantically indeterminate.

This indeterminacy, furthermore, has quite specific historical origins. The monolingual dictionary started life as a compilation of textual glosses; but in the process the glosses became decontextualized. Thus instead of providing interpretations of particular words in particular texts, the lexical entry acquired a generalized function of much wider and vaguer scope. That lexicographers themselves assign no specific limits to this semiological formula can be seen from the wide variation in its lexicographical use. For instance, one and the same modern dictionary (*Pocket Oxford Dictionary*, 5th edition, 1969) can provide entries like the following:

> *unwound : not wound*
> *spinach : plant with succulent leaves eaten boiled.*

(In both instances these are the sole glosses provided.) Now whatever view one takes of semantic relations, it seems clear that *unwound* does not stand to *not wound* as *spinach* stands to *plant with succulent leaves eaten boiled.* And if that variation is legitimate, there can be no question of attributing any specific value to the entry formula which provides a lexical lemma with a lexical gloss.

The difference might perhaps be described in different ways. For example, it might be urged that whereas *not wound* provides an 'exact definition' of *unwound,* the gloss *plant with succulent leaves eaten boiled* gives only a 'rough indication' of the meaning of *spinach.* But if that is the case, then clearly the lexical formula has no precise value or semantic function.

It also seems clear that there are quite different communicational presuppositions underlying the two glosses cited above. Giving *plant with succulent leaves eaten boiled* as an explanation of what *spinach* means harks back to the marginal glosses of ancient texts. The assumption is that *for present purposes* that is the kind of information required. So any modern who looked up the word in search of a precise botanical category is going to be disappointed. Such a person might indeed well complain that the gloss given is quite inadequate, or even wrong, given that there are many other kinds of plant with succulent leaves than spinach. On the other hand, no such objection is likely to be raised to glossing *unwound* as *not wound*. Here the objection is more likely to be that readers already familiar with the word *wound* are not likely to be looking up *unwound*, while those familiar with neither are not going to be enlightened anyway.

If these or similar comments are reasonable, it is difficult to maintain that there is any determinate semantic function attaching to the lexical formula or any specific semantic correlation that the lexicographer ought to have been trying to provide. Rather it seems more sensible to say that whether the correlations proposed are satisfactory or not will depend on whether the lexicographer has made the right communicational assumptions. In very general terms, one might describe those assumptions simply as being that the terms proposed in the gloss are likely to provide a more useful alternative than the term glossed. That does not necessarily mean, however, that they will be more familiar terms.

Again, there is a historical dimension to lexicography that is, from an integrational point of view, relevant to understanding current practice. The fact is that only relatively recently did common, everyday words get to be listed in monolingual dictionaries at all. The purpose of the first monolingual dictionaries in English was undoubtedly the modest one of explaining difficult, technical or unfamiliar words that readers might encounter. But then the notion arose that a dictionary ought to be 'complete', i.e. to include *all* words in the language, not just a selection of awkward ones. And this created a problem for lexicographers, because the technique of glossing the less familiar by the more familiar breaks down when dealing with words that everybody already knows. Lexicographers in fact tended to deal with this problem by standing it on its head. They assumed that what is needed by someone looking up some very familiar word must be a more recondite definition, reflecting expertise and specialist knowledge not available to the average reader. This is what leads to dictionary entries such as (*Pocket Oxford Dictionary* again):

> *bird : feathered vertebrate*

For it is scarcely credible that the number of people in the world familiar with the expression *feathered vertebrate* exceeds the number of those already familiar with the word *bird* and the creatures so designated.

In short, according to the integrationist, what is going on in the dictionary is a communicational process designed to cater for certain communicational needs, and designed to do so by proposing a reduction of semantic indeterminacy *in relation to these needs as perceived*. This is a far cry from segregationist theories of the dictionary, in which it is construed as a documentation of objectively ascertainable semantic relations.

But it is no part of the integrationist case to claim that lexicographers pluck words and glosses out of thin air: lexicographers are indeed sign-makers, but not conjurors. Lexicographers, like their clients, operate in the context of a linguistic community, just as a banker or a stockbroker operates in the context of a financial community. What the integrationist points out is that to represent the activity of the lexicographer as a mere reporting of semantic facts is rather like portraying the banker and the stockbroker as mere go-betweens in financial transactions engineered by other parties. The reality is somewhat different. The banker and the stockbroker are themselves key figures in creating the market they administer. They are not somehow outside it, looking on as impartial observers. Nor, *mutatis mutandis*, is the lexicographer.

Regulating meanings

The integrationist does not deny that for all kinds of purposes human beings may *attempt* to establish fixed communicational codes; and in many cases they do so successfully. In these cases we have examples of what may be called 'regulated determinacy'. But regulated determinacy is itself context-dependent. A familiar example is the traffic light system, which works on the whole very well. It is instrumental in making road travel much safer than it otherwise would be. Nor does the integrationist wish to deny that verbal signs may be subject to regulated determinacy, i.e. incorporated as elements in fixed codes (as, for example, the words *Give way* when appearing as part of a Highway Code traffic sign). The question of how far regulated determinacy can be pushed in the case of verbal signs is an interesting one. Technical terminology and its development provides an interesting area for study, particularly in relation to the reasons for which, in particular cases, it was considered desirable to arrive at agreed definitions. (Locke held this to be a pressing need and a *sine qua non* for the advancement of science. An integrationist would point out that Locke's concern presupposes that semantic indeterminacy is the rule for language in general.) The law is another rich field for investigation: what happens in courts, particularly nowadays, suggests that in the final analysis there is no verbal formulation whatsoever, however apparently precise, of which the meaning cannot be disputed.

The general point here is that successful fixed codes can operate only under limited conditions and in circumstances where there is a genuine consensus about their operation (including who is subject to them).

Furthermore, they quickly break down when the regulatory conditions are breached or become unenforceable (Harris, 1996c, pp.247ff.) It is a mistake to treat a language like English as a gigantic fixed code, for at least three reasons.

First, circumstances in which a genuine consensus could be established never obtain, because there are too many speakers and the inventory of potential linguistic signs is too large. In the second place, there is no effective social mechanism for guaranteeing regulation, even though governments and academies have sometimes tried to provide it. In the third place, even if it were politically possible, regulated determinacy of language in general would be counterproductive. For one of the important functions of communication is adaptation to new circumstances as and when they arise, which is all the time. Any monolithic fixed code with fixed meanings would be an enormous hindrance rather than a help in human affairs.

But there are also powerful psychological reasons why such an attempt would be doomed to failure.

Metaphor

One of these is that the human mind has an irrepressible capacity for creating new patterns out of whatever materials come to hand. This is seen in the linguistic phenomenon for which the traditional Western term is 'metaphor'. Metaphorical meaning is usually contrasted with 'literal' meaning. It is no coincidence that Aristotle, who was the first scholar to made any serious attempt to explain metaphor, was also one of the founders of a fixed-code theory of languages. For from a fixed-code perspective, metaphor is an aberration. It involves an 'improper' use of words. It applies terms to cases where they are not strictly or 'literally' applicable. It is a semantic deviation.

It is significant that Aristotle's account of metaphor occurs in his *Poetics*, which already classifies it implicitly as characteristic of a rather exceptional kind of discourse. His explanation constitutes the first known attempt to formulate a theory of semantic transference:

> Metaphor consists in giving the thing a name that belongs to something else; the transference being either from genus to species, or from species to genus, or from species to species, or on grounds of analogy. (*Poetics* 21)

The underlying logic of this explanation is typical of fixed-code semantics. First we have the assumption that a determinate correlation between names and things is already in place, such that each name has an identified thing 'belonging' to it. Second, we have the assumption that metaphor disrupts these correlations by giving a thing the 'wrong' name, i.e. a name that rightly belongs to some other thing. Third, we have the assumption that nevertheless this transference is systematic in some way, and an explanation of the phenomenon will consist in demonstrating its systematicity (genus to species, species to genus, etc.). Aristotle does not apparently see – or is not prepared to admit – that his first three categories of transfer are actually special cases of the fourth and most general: analogy. For if this were admitted, the systematicity would disappear, and one would be left with a conclusion intolerable to fixed-code theorists; namely, that the fixed code is not actually fixed. For users alter its name-thing correlations at will, as it tickles their fancy to do so.

Aristotle's location of this discussion in the *Poetics* also suggests that (to put the matter with deliberate anachronism) he wants to treat metaphor as a matter of *parole*, not of *langue*. Which is another favourite segregationist escape route for dealing with recalcitrant 'data'. This might be plausible if it were only poets or other eccentrics who indulged in such linguistic perversities. But what is even more disturbing for fixed-code semantics is that apparently deviations like metaphor can eventually worm their way into the code itself. Mountains do not have feet, but no eyebrows are raised when someone speaks of the 'foot of the Matterhorn'. Nor does it cause us any problem to work out what kind of animal a 'human guinea-pig' might be. Worse still, as soon as we start looking for metaphors we find them all over the place. They suddenly appear in even the most banal and commonplace of utterances.

The core problem here is, again, one generated by the fixed-code doctrine itself; the problem being that the distinction between the literal and the metaphorical melts away when we try to draw it in any systematic or rigorous way. (How many metaphors does the preceding sentence include?) And this problem in turn relates to another; what also melts away is the elusive distinction between the code and its use, between *langue* and *parole*. When we adopt an integrational perspective, we see that in fact these two difficulties are head and tail of the same theoretical coin.

The recommended integrationist approach to metaphor will already be apparent from the foregoing discussion: its starting point is to question 'whether metaphors are indeed different in kind from language use in general', this being no more than a corollary of the integrationist view that 'novelty in language use is the norm' (Toolan, 1996, pp.59-60). Once we accept that, contrary to what fixed-code theorists would have us believe, 'anything can mean anything in particular circumstances' (Toolan, 1996, p.62), then the question for investigation is how those particular circumstances produce the pattern of integration that results in *something* meaning what it does.

Meaning as doing

The question raised at the beginning of this chapter was: 'What is it that I don't know if I don't know what it means?' And the integrationist answer is: 'What you don't know is what to do with it.' This answer may at first sight appear to conflict with firmly and widely held lay convictions about what words mean (particularly if we have been brought up to believe in the sacrosanctity of the dictionary). But this apparent conflict disappears when we consider more carefully the issues involved.

To anyone who feels inclined to protest that merely using an already familiar word in an unexceptional way does not entail any creation of new meaning by the user, the integrationist reply is: 'Yes, it does: that is precisely what it requires.' For using a word, in the sense in which semantics is concerned with the use of words, is not a matter of random instantiation, or of simply mouthing certain sounds, or inscribing certain marks on paper. It involves using the word meaningfully, which in turn means using it in certain circumstances for a certain communicational purpose. Once this point is firmly grasped, there can be no question of denying the user's role as a maker of meaning. For to use a word in this sense we have to make it mean something. To try to use a word without making it meaningful would be as absurd as trying to use a knife without cutting anything, or a hammer without banging anything. (If the objection is raised that knives and hammers can also be used for such varied purposes as propping open windows or stubbing out cigarettes, the short answer to that is that in those cases they are not being used *as* knives or hammers.)

Using a word is making it mean something, and making it mean something is *doing* something with it; but not just in the sense of the title of J.L. Austin's *How to do things with Words*. (On the relationship between integrationism and Austin's position, see Love, 1997.) Too hasty an acceptance of Austin's celebrated distinction between 'performative' and 'constative' might mislead the unwary into supposing that we are only *doing* things with words when we make apologies, promises, or perform some similar speech act of a more or less ritualized kind that has a recognized metalinguistic designation. But this is not the integrationist's interpretation. Doing things with words involves integrating them into a communication process. And we cannot do that without considering the biomechanical, macrosocial and circumstantial conditions of each particular case.

It is also important, as far as the integrationist is concerned, to realize that it is not only speakers and writers but listeners and readers who do things with words and are thus involved in their use. To understand a word – and not just an unfamiliar word like *moshpit* but a familar word like, say, *bicycle* – I have to make it mean something (even if I have all kinds of doubts and hesitations about what I make it mean). Part of

Humpty Dumpty's mistake was that he thought the speaker was in charge of meaning and the listener (Alice, in this instance) had to defer to the speaker's intentions. (A remarkably similar thesis sometimes surfaces in modern literary criticism.) But, as has already been mentioned above, intentions are not to be confused with meanings, even though it makes sense to say 'I did not mean that' in order to deny that you intended it, and even though intentions of some kind are required in order to make words mean anything at all. The conflation of what is meant with what is intended is a serious source of confusion in contemporary semantics, and has close connexions with the fallacy of telementation, on which it is based. For the integrationist, setting aside both is an essential first step in the demythologization of meaning.

Further reading

- Harris and Wolf, 1998, Part 3, 'Language and Meaning'
- On metaphor: Harris and Taylor, 1997, Ch. 2; Toolan, 1996, Ch. 2
- On meaning and intention: Harris, 1996c, Ch. 4; Toolan 1996, Ch. 3
- On truth: Harris, 1981b; Harris, 1996b, Ch.7

Questions for discussion

1. Consider the following statements and discuss how an integrationist might respond to them:
(a) 'We can define the meaning of a speech-form accurately when this meaning has to do with some matter of which we possess scientific knowledge.' (L. Bloomfield)
(b) 'The person who has acquired knowledge of a language has internalized a system of rules that relate sound and meaning in a particular way.' (N. Chomsky)
(c) 'In the primary speech situation 'meaning' is as much a property of the situational context of people, things, and events as of the 'noise' made by the speaker.' (J.R. Firth)
(d) 'The meaning of a word is something inherent in it.' (A.H. Gardiner)
(e) 'All definitions are essentially *ad hoc*.' (C.K. Ogden and I.A. Richards)
(f) 'Meaning is what essence becomes when it is divorced from the object of reference and wedded to the word.' (W.V.O. Quine)
2. Glossing practices, both formal and informal, employ a wide range of devices. They are often overtly signalled in discourse by metalinguistic markers like 'in other words' or 'that is to say'. How many can you identify in the preceding chapter?

4

Language and Discourse

The term 'discourse' is used by integrationists to apply to a much wider range of phenomena than in orthodox linguistics. It covers spoken and written communication and both verbal and non-verbal communication as well. Whereas the 'talking heads' model restricts *parole* to what *A* and *B* say and hear, excluding any other activities such as gaze, gesture, physical contact (e.g. shaking hands), etc., the integrationist will include all these as integrated components of the exchange taking place, and will justify this inclusion by pointing out that, in isolation from the rest, the words uttered would in many cases fail to make much sense at all. This is particularly so where *A* and *B* are engaged in some joint enterprise, to the execution of which their talk is directed.

Thus for the integrationist it is the contextualized integration of utterances into other activities which produces (spoken) discourse. This stands in sharp contrast to the very restricted use of the term 'discourse' in orthodox linguistics, where it often means no more than 'a set of utterances which constitute any recognizable speech event' (Crystal, 1991, p.106). This not only confines discourse to spoken discourse but even appears reluctant to admit that the addressee (as distinct from the speaker) takes part in it at all.

Discourse and context

The embedding of speech in other activities was first emphasized in linguistics by Malinowski, who put forward what he called an 'ethnographic theory of language'. One of Malinowski's main tenets is that language is a 'mode of action' rather than a 'countersign of thought'

(Malinowski, 1923, p.296). He adds, however, the qualification 'in its primitive function'. In his view, the linguistics of his day ('the philological approach to language') had failed to give adequate recognition to 'the pragmatic character of language' and had been 'largely vitiated' by its 'false conception of language as a means of transfusing ideas from the head of the speaker to that of the listener' (Malinowski, 1935, ii, p.9). Here we have as outright a condemnation of the telementational fallacy as any integrationist would wish for.

An integrationist would also endorse Malinowski's contention that 'the utterance has no meaning except in the context of situation' (Malinowski, 1923, p.307), while nevertheless having reservations about what Malinowski understood by 'context' (Wolf, 1989). For in the end it seems that Malinowski could not bring himself to give up the notion that words have determinate meanings after all; and at that point Malinowski's perspective diverges from the integrationist's. For Malinowski, the 'primitive function' of language is to be contrasted with its 'developed literary and scientific functions', where he concedes it to be 'an instrument of thought and of the communication of thought' (Malinowski, 1923, p.297). For an integrationist, on the other hand, if language is a 'mode of action' at all, then it is a mode of action all the time, and not just in its 'primitive function' (whatever that might be). It is difficult to see, in fact, why Malinowski does not count 'the communication of thought' as a form of action, in the same way as, for example, does Pinker, who claims that by means of speech 'we can shape events in each other's brains with exquisite precision'. More explicitly still, 'simply by making noises with our mouths, we can reliably cause new combinations of ideas to arise in each other's minds' (Pinker, 1994, p.14). Deliberately causing something to happen is nothing if not taking action; and, in the case of *A* speaking to *B*, fairly direct action with immediate effect.

The question an integrationist would want to put to both Pinker and Malinowski is why such emphasis should be laid from the outset on the difference between the kind of action that merely has mental consequences (provoking 'thoughts') and the kind of action that has various other physiological or physical consequences (either instead of or in addition to the mental consequences). The answer is fairly clear. Those who think of languages in these terms, however sophisticated their terminology, are still in the grip of the telementational fallacy that mesmerized Locke and many of his predecessors in the Western tradition. That is why, on the one hand, they pay attention only to those parts of the 'speech circuit' that are supposedly instrumental in linking up the thought in *A*'s mind to the thought in *B*'s mind (often construing the connexion, explicitly in Pinker's case, as *causal*); and, on the other hand, why they treat the context as a mere physical 'setting' which provides a stage for the action but is not part of it.

The nearest that orthodox linguistics comes to erasing this division is in admitting preceding and following speech as part of 'context', although in some terminologies this is explicitly distinguished from context by calling it 'co-text' (Crystal, 1991, p.87). But all these manœuvres have the underlying aim, clearly, of maintaining as segregated domains the study of the 'linguistic' features and the study of the accompanying 'non-linguistic' or 'extra-linguistic' features. The belief that such a distinction can be coherently drawn and is universally valid is still the underlying segregationist article of faith. So much so that one sometimes finds integrational linguistics described as an approach which considers language 'in terms of a wide range of phenomena, both linguistic and non-linguistic' (Figueroa, 1994, p.21). By now, a reader of this book should not need to have it explained why an integrationist might find this description amusing.

Theories of context

When Firth took over Malinowski's notion of context, he proposed a typology in which various contexts were regarded as nested one within another, as in a Chinese box. The 'outermost' context was what Firth called the 'context of culture', within which various types of 'context of situation' were to be distinguished, and within these the 'context of experience' of the participants, and so on, down to the innermost context, which was the 'phonetic context' (Firth, 1957a, p.36). For Firth, the 'phonetic context' was rock bottom: there was no further or lower level of context at which speech events occurred. Firth held that when any speech event had been analysed in such a way that its components had been exhaustively described in terms of the various contexts in which they occurred, there was nothing more for the linguist to say about it; and this approach to linguistic description he proposed as preferable to having to postulate 'an elaborate mental structure such as is derived from de Saussure'. The linguist would simply give 'a serial contextualization of our facts, context within context, each one being a function, an organ of the bigger context and all contexts finding a place in what may be called the context of culture'. This would avoid 'many of the difficulties which arise if meaning is regarded as a mental relation' (Firth, 1957a, p.32). It is evident from this last remark that Firth saw his theory of context as providing a way of doing linguistics without subscribing to the language myth.

Any such attempt an integrationist will *pro tanto* approve. But although a number of Firth's pronouncements have an integrationist ring to them, including the iconoclastic dictum that 'each word when used in a new context is a new word' (Firth, 1957a, p.190), his theory of context does not provide what an integrationist is looking for. In the first place, it throws out the baby of communication with the bathwater of telementation. In other words, it is far from clear how Firth's technique of 'serial contextualization' explicates or even leaves room for the notion that speech events are part of a communication process; for presumably all human behaviour, whether communicational or not, takes place within some outer 'context of culture' and could be analysed in terms of a progressively more restricted series of inner contexts, appropriately selected. Firth does not tell us at what contextual level communication enters the picture. In the second place, Firth seems no less committed than Saussure to the linguistic/non-linguistic dichotomy and to a strictly phonocentric version of it. For the lowest-level elements that are 'contextualized' in Firth's system are always individual speech-sounds of 'a language'. How these units are identified in the first place we are not told: Firth seems to take them as 'given', although admitting that 'no two people pronounce exactly alike' (Love, 1988). Third, Firth originally insisted on the necessity of ensuring that what the linguist is studying are the 'facts of speech' (Firth, 1957a, p.35: paper published in 1934). He says that these 'facts' must be taken 'from speech sequences, verbally complete in themselves and operating in contexts of situation which are typical, recurrent, and repeatedly observable'. But where these assurances of completeness, typicality, recurrence and observability are to come from is entirely unclear: how the linguist is to know what counts as 'the same context again' remains a central and unresolved problem. It seems pointless to proclaim that 'each word when used in a new context is a new word' if there is no way of distinguishing between a new context and an old one. Later in his career, Firth took a more sceptical view of the 'facts' of speech.

> It is unnecessary to assume any 'facts' prior to statement. No fact is merely itself so to speak. There are no brute facts. A fact has to be stated in technical language at each level for each technique and for each discipline. An isolate is always an abstraction from the language complex which is itself abstracted from the mush of general goings-on. (Firth, 1957b, p.29)

Although this looks at first sight like a welcome change from the naive faith in linguistic 'data' evinced by so many linguists of the twentieth century, it does not make Firth's position on contexts any easier to accept. Particularly when juxtaposed to the immediately following claim:

> Attested language text duly recorded is in the focus of attention for the linguist. In dealing with such texts abstracted from the matrix of experience most of the environmental accompaniment in the mush of general goings-on must of necessity be suppressed. (Firth, 1957b, pp.29-30)

For here it looks as though the contexts are just as much conjured up out of the 'mush' by the linguist as the 'texts' and the 'facts': their existence is also due to what the linguist has decided to 'suppress' or not to 'suppress'.

A theory of context no less complex than Firth's is proposed by Hymes. Hymes not only speaks of the need 'to investigate directly the use of language in contexts of situation' but goes much further than many theorists in detailing the possible features of the context. He calls these 'components of speech acts' and lists sixteen. They are, in his terminology: (i) message form, (ii) message content, (iii) setting, (iv) scene (or 'psychological setting'), (v) speaker, (vi) addressor, (vii) hearer, (viii) addressee, (ix) purposes-outcomes, (x) purposes-goals, (xi) key, (xii) channel, (xiii) form of speech, (xiv) norm of interaction, (xv) norm of interpretation, and (xvi) genre (Hymes, 1974, pp.53-66). These are not envisaged as internally nested layers of context, as in Firth's scheme, but seem rather to be an inventory of all the types of factor that Hymes considers might possibly affect the production or interpretation of a speech act. If that is so, an integrationist would point out that since almost anything from the time of day to the height above sea level might, in particular circumstances, have such an effect, it seems highly arbitrary to reduce the list of possibilities to sixteen.

Hymes does speak, however, of working towards 'an integrated approach to linguistic description'. But he proposes the following gloss on 'integrated': that it be taken to

> encompass the structure of sentences within the structure of discourse, of referential meaning within the meanings of speech acts, and of dialects and languages within the organization of verbal repertoires and speech communities. (Hymes, 1974, p.195)

This seems to be ambiguous as between two possible readings: (i) that sentences, referential meanings, dialects and languages are merely abstractions from discourse, speech acts, verbal repertoires, etc. and should be recognized as such, or (ii) that the former are components of the latter, which 'contextualize' them, i.e. constitute the larger complexes in terms of which former have to be understood. With the first of these propositions an integrationist would have some sympathy, but the second is no more than a compromise with segregational linguistics.

Finally, mention must be made here of the 'interactional sociolinguistic' position on context taken by J.J. Gumperz. Gumperz writes:

> The linguistic character of contextualization cues is such that they are uninterpretable apart from concrete situations. In contrast to words or segmental morphemes which, although ultimately also context-bound, can at least be discussed in

> isolation [...] contextualization phenomena are impossible to describe in abstract terms. (Gumperz, 1982, p.170)

This sounds like something an integrationist would be prepared to accept. But what Gumperz offers with his right hand is speedily withdrawn by his left. He maintains that, in spite of the impossibility of describing contextualization phenomena 'in abstract terms', nevertheless there are public 'contextualization conventions' about which the linguist can gather 'strong evidence' by 'looking at systematic patterns in the relationship of perception of surface cues to interpretation' (Gumperz, 1982, p.170). This move immediately takes us back to Firth's unresolved problem of detecting recurrent contexts of situation. Furthermore, it appears to presuppose that the connexion between 'cue' and 'interpretation' is somehow open to inspection; whereas an integrationist would point out that it is far from clear that participants themselves always know which particular details or combinations of details in an episode of communication led them to interpret it as they did (McGregor, 1986).

The approaches to context discussed above comprise only a fraction of the numerous proposals on this topic that have been put forward by different theorists. They have been selected here because they are sometimes taken as reflecting or being close to the integrationist position on context. However, the integrationist position is radically different from any of these.

Contextualization and cotemporality

For the integrationist, contextualization, like all other aspects of communication, is subject to the principle of cotemporality. This means that, to put it in Heraclitan terms, 'one cannot step into the same context twice' (McDonough, 1993, p.152), any more than into the same river. Or, for the integrationist, any more than one can say 'the same thing over again' (Ch. 3, pp.53ff.).

In his discussion of the Heraclitan view of context, McDonough cites Wittgenstein's remark: 'If we look at the actual use of a word, what we see is something constantly fluctuating' (Wittgenstein, 1974, p.77). Wittgenstein goes on to observe that when we investigate language we 'set over against this fluctuation something more fixed, just as one paints a stationary picture of the constantly altering face of the landscape'. One thinks immediately of 'something more fixed' that appears between the covers of a dictionary. Does Wittgenstein mean that we cannot investigate language *without* making the kinds of assumption about dealing with determinate forms and meanings that a lexicographer makes, and that unless we are willing to pay this price, to accept this degree of falsification, then we must renounce any hope of doing linguistics at all?

If so, Wittgenstein is mounting a more powerful defence of segregationism than any linguist has ever succeeded in doing, and therefore one that the integrationist cannot afford to ignore. McDonough concludes that in linguistics, or at least in philosophy of linguistics, it is important to 'define a sense in which the context can remain the same [...] but another sense in which the context, and so the meaning, is constantly changing'. An integrationist will say that integrationism allows us to meet both those challenges (although not perhaps exactly in the way McDonough appears to envisage).

It is interesting to ask why Wittgenstein chooses to compare the investigation of language with painting a landscape, as opposed to taking a photograph of a landscape. The answer that suggests itself is that he wished to emphasize the idea that capturing exactly the appearance of the landscape at one moment is, for the painter, out of the question: the paint cannot be applied to the canvas fast enough. Both the changes in the landscape and what the painter is doing are parallel sequences in 'real time' and one cannot 'catch up' with the other. In other words, Wittgenstein not only recognizes the principle of cotemporality but recognizes it as applying *both* to our verbal activities *and* to our intellectual inquiry into those activities. The analogy of photography would not serve this purpose, precisely because the photographer has a machine which enables an 'instantaneous' view to be captured. (Whether the human eye ever sees the landscape as the camera 'sees' it is another question.)

What, then, does the painter's picture actually show? Does it 'record' anything at all? This is the key question if the parallel between painting and investigating language is to be taken seriously.

Various answers might be proposed. The answer most in line with integrationist thinking is one which treats the picture as a creative construction by the painter. This construction is based not only on what the painter sees – or saw a few moments ago – but on many previous experiences of looking at landscapes *and painting*. It is, furthermore, a construction which reflects the painter's current interest in certain aspects of visual experience and certain features of this landscape; for no painting can capture everything visible. It may also reflect much else, depending on the purpose for which the painting is being executed, the taste of potential buyers, etc. In short, the painting is itself a contextualized product of the integration of past, present and projected future activities by the painter. This too is subject to various biomechanical, macrosocial and circumstantial conditions, as all human communication is. Furthermore – and this is perhaps the most important point – the integration of the activities in question actually affects and is crucial to the production: the painter looks at the landscape with a different eye when painting. Recontextualizing the landscape is a *sine qua non* for painting it. That is why some painters are content to paint 'the same subject' over and over again; it is not because they are never satisfied with their efforts to capture it 'exactly'.

Contextualization and reflexivity

Where Wittgenstein's analogy breaks down, for the integrationist, is over the role of the painter's materials and tools. Applying paint from palette to canvas by means of brushes is a quite independent and artificial second-order enterprise which has only a contingent relationship with the first-order visual experience of the landscape. But in the linguistic case, by contrast, no other tools are available for language-painting than those already supplied by language. In linguistics, as Firth rightly remarked, 'language is turned back upon itself' (Firth, 1957a, p.147). Firth saw this as 'one of our major problems' but, as Love points out, although occasionally drawing attention to it, Firth did not know what to make of it (Love, 1988, p.164).

The reflexivity of language is what makes linguistic description a fundamentally different enterprise from painting a landscape. This does not invalidate Wittgenstein's analogy entirely, but once we are aware of it – as Wittgenstein undoubtedly was – it puts the analogy in a somewhat different light. (It rules out, for instance, such naive interpretations as that Wittgenstein thought that linguistic change was proceeding at such a rate as to render synchronic descriptions out of date before publication.)

Where the integrationist differs from Firth is in supposing that language is 'turned back upon itself' *not only* in linguistics but in the activities of everyday discourse (and, further, in supposing that failure to realize this is at the bottom of major inadequacies of modern linguistics). If we grant that Wittgenstein, too, recognized the pervasive reflexivity of language, it would follow that we are intended to construe the landscape-painting analogy along integrationist lines. In other words, it would be absurd for the painter to think that speeding up the brushwork will solve the problem. An intelligent painter will see from the beginning that in choosing to paint the landscape, what has been chosen is the production of a static image of a fluctuating reality. And if this is unacceptable, then some different kind of image must be sought instead (cinematographic, for example?). But for the painter *qua* painter, there is no other option. It is not difficult to translate this to the case of linguistic inquiry. Wittgenstein seems indeed to be alluding here to the reflexivity of language, and specifically to the problem of metalanguage. His point is that we can be deceived by the metalinguistic terms and concepts we are forced to use for purposes of linguistic inquiry into thinking that they correspond to categories as unproblematic for all practical purposes as *cat, dog, house*, etc. and all the familiar apparatus of our non-metalinguistic talk. But this is a metalinguistic illusion, just as the painter's static image of the fluctuating landscape is a kind of metavisual illusion.

This interpretation of Wittgenstein's view finds support in his immediately following remark:

> When we study language we *envisage* it as a game with fixed rules. We compare it with, and measure it against, a game of that kind. (Wittgenstein, 1974, p.77)

Here Wittgenstein is plainly referring to the familiar fixed-code view of the Western tradition; but it is the preceding painting analogy which carries the interesting suggestion that perhaps the source of this readiness to envisage language as 'a game with fixed rules' is the way metalanguage leads us to accept an image of the word as a static object. It is interesting that these remarks of Wittgenstein's date from the early 1930s, at a time when fixed-code linguistics was becoming entrenched in European and American universities as the 'scientific' approach to the study of language. But by the time he wrote *Philosophical Investigations* Wittgenstein had moved to a view of language in which we are invited to see the word as deriving its meaning from communicational integration within a programme of activity. The simple four-word builder's language described at the beginning of the latter work is one where the builder simply calls out 'Block!', 'Pillar!', 'Slab!' or 'Beam!', as the case may, and his assistant fetches the appropriate item at each call (Wittgenstein, 1953, §2). This could almost stand as an illustrative working model of Malinowski's theory of language as a 'mode of action'. Each call from the builder must move the process along one stage further. It is not sufficient merely to trigger some 'concept' in the assistant's mind.

But if this 'primitive language' is not to be interpreted as merely reinstating the familiar fixed-code conception of a communication system, in which each of four vocal signs has a determinate form and meaning for both builder and assistant, it is essential that we see Wittgenstein's point as being that the *only* determinacy is provided by the context of activity, i.e. by the ongoing building programme. That is to say, the production of signs in discourse can fluctuate up to any limit that does not disrupt that programme. Since the builder and his assistant do not have a metalanguage (Wittgenstein deliberately stipulates: 'Conceive this as a complete primitive language'), they cannot renegotiate either the details or the principles of the system other than by some process of give-and-take in the activity of discourse itself. But here discourse has to include, as the integrationist would insist, the non-vocal part of their interaction.

The example, although a philosophical fiction, enables one to see very clearly how the integrationist concept of discourse links up with rejection of the language myth. Whereas the segregationist treats discourse as comprising simply the builder's utterances, and 'the language' as consisting of the four words that constitute the invariant types ('*block*', '*pillar*', '*slab*', '*beam*') of which these utterances are tokens, the integrationist sees the assistant's activities of seeking and fetching the required items as no less constitutive of discourse. Going and fetching a block in response to the builder's call is no less a linguistic act than the utterance 'Block!' which prompted it. The integration of the two is precisely what is necessary to the operation of a communication system.

Text and context

Texts occur in contexts. Or do they? Two quite different interpretations of what a text is have to be distinguished. According to one of these, a text is simply a stretch of discourse located by reference to a certain context. On the other interpretation, a text is already a context-free abstraction; as, for example, when 'the text' of a poem is cited without any reference to its author, date and place of composition, etc. Both of these are metalinguistic constructions, in the sense that they involve very different ways of identifying and discussing linguistic phenomena, and thus projecting and legitimizing very different kinds of question about them.

As far as the integrationist is concerned, there is no acceptance that 'text and context are distinct and stable categories, prior to consideration of particular cases' (Toolan, 1996, p.4). Or, more explicitly still, 'there really is no such thing as *the* context' (Toolan, 1996, p.4). For the integrationist, context is not a 'given': it is a product of contextualization. And contextualization cannot be divorced from the recognition of the sign. 'Signification and contextualization are not two independent elements but facets of the same creative activity' (Harris, 1996c, p.164).

In order to flesh out generalizations of this kind it may be useful to consider a specific but typical case in which the question of situating 'a text' in its 'context' arises. Students are often asked to explain a text by reference to information which it 'takes for granted' but does not make explicit. For example, the following epigram by Evelyn Waugh is discussed in these terms by Gerald Guinness (Guinness, 1980):

> *Trusty as steel, more valuable than plate,*
> *Aspiring Sheffield knocked at Heaven's gate.*
> *Top Man, who reads The Times, pronounced his doom,*
> *Coldly remarking: "Stanley, I presume?"*

In order to understand this short poem, it is necessary, as Guinness points out, to know a great deal. And the further the reader is from the actual circumstances which occasioned its composition, the more remote and inaccessible this knowledge seems. The orthodox 'contextual' explanation would run as follows: the context of the poem is that an English nobleman, Lord Stanley of Alderley, decided for reasons best known to himself that he did not wish to be called 'Lord Stanley of Alderley' any longer, and so caused a discreet notice to appear in *The Times* announcing that henceforth Lord Stanley of Alderley wished to be known by the title of his senior barony as 'Lord Sheffield'.

For Waugh, evidently, this little episode epitomized the outdated pretentiousness of a certain upper-class stratum of British society of the post-war period: hence the poem. But as time goes by, the poem presents a problem to readers for whom less and less of the relevant facts are available as matters of 'common knowledge': for instance, that Sheffield is a town in England famous, or once famous, for its manufacture of cutlery; that an English peer can inherit several titles but will be known formally only by the title of his choice – in this case the senior (that is, oldest) barony; that there was a famous episode in the exploration of Africa when, after months of search, Henry Stanley found the explorer David Livingstone near the headwaters of the Congo and greeted him with the words 'Dr Livingstone, I presume?'.

These, Guinness observes, are public facts that a diligent student who happened to be ignorant of them could nevertheless discover by assiduous research in the appropriate works of reference. (Guinness does not say how the student would discover that these facts were indeed relevant to the intepretation of the poem; but this we may leave on one side for the moment.)

However, there are further pertinent facts that are not so easily recoverable from works of reference. Prominent among these is the fact that during the late 1950s *The Times* ran a series of advertising campaigns which proclaimed to the public at large the message 'Top People read *The Times*'. The accompanying illustrations identified these 'top people' as judges, bankers, tycoons, etc. Perhaps, Guinness admits, a really determined researcher could even discover that.

But then we come to things that are not a matter of public record as such, but depend more on a certain feeling for attitudes and relationships. For instance, how natural it would seem for a certain class of English person to assume that if God read a newspaper at all, it would be *The Times*. Or to assume that members of the House of Lords would not, in the normal course of events, be kept waiting at the Pearly Gates while their identity was checked. Or the casting of God in the role of super-snob, which, says Guinness, 'acquires a certain piquancy from Waugh's own very snobbish brand of convert-Catholicism'.

Much more could be said about this example. But the points an integrationist would wish to draw attention to are these. 1. Different types of audience and different individual readers may be expected to vary in respect of the amount of 'context' which they need to have 'supplied' (e.g. in the way of footnotes to the poem) in order to make sense of it, as distinct from what they take for granted. 2. It would be impossible to draw up a definitive list of items which constituted the 'essential context' for this poem. Or rather, any attempt to do so would automatically blur any distinction between linguistic and non-linguistic knowledge. Are there readers to whom it would be necessary to explain 'God' and 'Heaven's gate'? Or why 'steel' should be 'trusty'? Or are these words assumed, as it were, to embody the relevant answers as part of their discursive function? Such questions are unanswerable.

All this points to a conclusion which an integrationist might formulate as follows. What is 'in the text' and outside it will vary from reader to reader. And even from one occasion of reading to the next if, in the interim, the reader has acquired more information, or certain points have meanwhile 'sunk in'. Which is to say that 'the text' itself is not a stable entity. We construct our texts as we go: they are not given to us in advance of the operations by which we contextualize them.

One further point – and perhaps the most important – may be made in reference to this example and its bearing on the integrationist concept of discourse. As Guinness observes, by the time all the contextual information supposedly necessary to appreciate Waugh's epigram has been spelt out (whether in the form of footnotes or by other means) the epigram itself is 'sprawled lifeless on the floor'. Which leads us to a paradox: analysis has actually destroyed what it apparently set out to explicate. What lesson should we learn from this?

The lesson the integrationist learns is that 'context' is not some specific set of background facts which contribute to, or are presupposed by, this or that episode of communication. By the same token, contextualization is not a laborious detailing of such information (except by the research student annotating the poem). Contextualization, in the example under consideration, is what integrates the verbal and non-verbal components of this episode into what Guinness describes as 'a mordant and witty joke'. But *that* view of Waugh's epigram requires the first-order engagement of an audience, not the second-order engagement of the analyst. And there might be different rationales, for different audiences, about what is funny. To that extent, we would be dealing with different jokes: hence different texts. There is an important difference between seeing *why* a joke is funny and actually finding it funny. (One can find it funny without understanding why, or understand what is funny about it without finding it funny oneself.) That difference is also a difference of contextualization in the integrationist sense. Once again, discourse is not reducible to the implementation of a fixed code. Except perhaps in some hypothetically homogeneous community where, *mirabile dictu*, all members share the same (genetically programmed?) sense of humour.

Context and understanding

Within an integrational framework, the challenge of finding a solution to the Heraclitan problem of stepping into the same context twice is not difficult to meet. The context will be 'the same' when it is perceived by the participants as being 'the same' in communicationally relevant respects. But that perception, clearly, may vary from one participant to another. Consider how a conversation between *A* and *B* might be affected by the arrival of *C*. Depending on the relationships between the three persons, on the topic of conversation, on the relevance of that topic to the continuance of the conversation, on whether *C* was expected, etc., *C*'s arrival might or might not be perceived as creating a new context. Or it might do so for *A* but not *B*, depending on their respective willingness to say certain things in *C*'s presence, etc. All conversation involves an ongoing process of contextualization and recontextualization of discourse by the participants. A single remark may suffice to 'change the context' or to prompt a reassessment of everything that has been said hitherto. The 'same context' is a function of that continuous monitoring of discourse that participation in discourse itself requires. All one can say in general is that certain changes in the biomechanical, macrosocial and circumstantial conditions might well be expected to provoke a recontextualization, and some almost certainly will.

Given the integrational treatment of context as *part of* – and not a setting for – discourse, there are important consequences for the notion of 'understanding'. Just as the integrationist will not construe understanding as something that depends on *B*'s grasping the same concept that *A* 'transmitted' by means of a fixed code, there is an analogous refusal to fall into the trap of setting up for the analysis of discourse 'any attempted inventory of conversational acts which stipulates entirely context-free correlations of particular utterances with particular conversational purposes' (Toolan, 1998). To approach discourse in this way would be simply to extend the fixed-code model at one remove, *even if* the scope of 'discourse' were enlarged to include various aspects of accompanying non-verbal behaviour. For an integrationist, the open-endedness of discourse is its most important characteristic. So 'understanding' itself is subject to the principle of cotemporality, i.e. is limited by what, at any given time, participants are aware of and how they contextualize this in relation to past and (projected) future experience.

A related point is made by Taylor when he observes that although people commonly assume that what they say is 'understood', and can produce reasons for this belief, nevertheless 'the ways in which speakers justify claims that their utterances have been understood are heavily dependent both on the contexts in which those utterances were produced as well as on the contexts in which their justifications are produced' (Taylor, 1998). He concludes that it is illusory for the linguist or the discourse analyst to embark on a search for some general set of 'assertion-conditions' to underpin assertions of the form 'H understood U' (where H = 'hearer' and U = 'utterance'), since these are not determinable in any context-neutral way.

A linguist reluctant to abandon so swiftly the possibility of making valid generalizations about 'understanding' discourse (perhaps because giving up generalizations is seen as tantamount to renouncing the possibility of 'scientific' investigation of the subject?) might be inclined to raise any or all of the following objections: (i) that Taylor's scepticism about decontextualized generalization conflicts with his apparent readiness to produce a generalization of his own (i.e. that we cannot generalize over criteria for 'understanding'), (ii) that the effect of this scepticism is to take us in a historical circle back to exactly the problem about communication that Locke formulated with such devastating effect (albeit on different grounds from Locke's), and (iii) that even if integrationists are right in calling in question the notion that there are 'rules' which relate discourse to understanding in any strictly determinate way, nevertheless it is not impossible that there are 'probabilistic' correlations to be discovered that will apply in the general run of cases.

How might an integrationist reply?

Objection (i) rests on an equivocation about 'generalization'. The thesis that there are no general 'assertion-conditions' for statements to the effect that *B* understands what *A* said is not arrived at by examining a large corpus of attested cases and trying to formulate some sustainable (although negative) conclusion (as, for example, one might conclude that British monarchs never produce Siamese twins as heirs to the throne). It is based on an argument about the way people produce justifications for their own beliefs about what has – or has not – been understood. One may, doubtless, reject this argument: but it is not rejected by pointing out that it yields a negative generalization.

Objection (ii) draws a misleading parallel between Locke's position and the integrationist's. Locke's scepticism about communication is a direct consequence of his own (fixed-code) assumptions about the criteria that need to be satisfied in discourse for understanding to occur. The integrationist position relativizes understanding discourse to contextualization, i.e. to the contextualization that participants carry out as a condition for engaging in discourse at all.

Objection (iii) is a placebo for linguists of a positivist disposition. But it does not work. Inserting the safeguard 'probably' will indeed get any theorist off the hook of claiming too much. Doubtless if *A* shakes his fist in *B*'s face, *B* will probably 'understand' this (rightly) as a gesture of hostility. For the mathematically fastidious, it might be feasible to assign some statistical value to the probability, allowing for variation between one community or cultural tradition and another. Research councils might even be persuaded to allocate grants for empirical investigation into the possibility that this gesture might turn out to be a 'universal' of human communication. But all this misses the integrationist point, which is not about the *prevalence* of certain correlations between form and understanding in discourse, but about the criteria for the correlations themselves. It is rather like confusing the weather forecast with a claim about the conditions under which barometric pressure corresponds to rainfall.

What falls within the scope of (spoken) 'discourse' is, for the integrationist, dependent in part on the claims that can be made about it. Claims to 'understand' what was said are among these. But here we come back to the reflexivity of language. Claims to understanding are metalinguistic claims. In Wittgenstein's builder's language no such claims can be formulated. The builder cannot say to his assistant, 'You did not understand what I said'; because they have no metalanguage. Nor can the assistant retort 'Yes, I did.' Does this mean they have no concept of understanding? Or does it mean merely that they cannot express that concept verbally? Or does it mean that in such a limited form of discourse as Wittgenstein describes, the question of understanding just does not arise, does not make sense, is an irrelevance, etc.?

These are not merely questions about Wittgenstein's example, but questions which probe 'our' concept of understanding and its relationship to 'displaying understanding' as a contribution to discourse. Insofar as 'our' concept of understanding implicates and is part of a communicational proficiency that depends on the availability of certain metalinguistic resources, the builder and his assistant plainly do not have it. We can say, if we like, that they have a surrogate for this concept, albeit of an impoverished kind, if we are willing to grant that they know when an instruction has been properly carried out and when it has not been carried out. And it must presumably be granted that they *do* know this if we are to make any sense at all of Wittgenstein's example. That is to say, if the assistant responded at random to the builder's instructions, and the builder for his part simply carried on with whatever material the assistant happened to bring, then the 'primitive language' Wittgenstein describes would not be in operation. But it would be illusory to suppose that a metalanguage adequate for displaying understanding can easily be supplied as an optional extra at no additional cost (i.e. cost in terms of complicating the cycle of operations). In this sense there is never any 'free' metalanguage in human communication.

Let us suppose, for instance, that in addition to the four words *block*, *pillar*, *slab* and *beam* the language has a fifth word **understood**. This is used by the assistant in response to the builder's giving an instruction. So, for instance, when the builder calls 'Block!' the assistant says 'Understood!' before going off to fetch a block. Does the language now have the metalanguage requisite for displaying understanding? We need to know more about what difference the incorporation of the new word makes to the rest of the activities in which the builder and his assistant are engaged. The fact that this addition to the vocabulary corresponds to the English verb *understand* is neither here nor there. It would not matter if the fifth word were *understood* or *rhubarb*: what matters is its integrational function. And if it makes no difference at all, in the sense that builder and his assistant otherwise carry on just as before, so that saying 'Understood!' (or 'Rhubarb!') simply becomes an automatic part of the assistant's execution of his duties, then we are still dealing with a communication system that lacks reflexivity.

To insist that saying 'Understood!' *does* display understanding on condition that the assistant only says it if he *has* understood does not advance matters. For the understanding that is germane to the building operation is that displayed by the assistant *in fetching* the required item: saying in addition 'Understood!' or 'Rhubarb!' or anything else is mere vocal redundancy unless its being said or not being said has consequences for other activities in the cycle.

Further reading

- Harris and Wolf, 1998, Part 4, 'Language and Discourse'
- On conversation: Taylor and Cameron, 1987

Questions for discussion

1. 'Even though not all utterances can be understood without attending to the particular discourse in which they occur or without attending to the context of utterance, there are nonetheless an indeterminate number of utterances that can be so understood.' (P. Ziff) What would an integrationist say to this?

2. 'Text and context are complementary.' (J. Lyons) But can we always distinguish which is which?

3. 'We rely upon our intuitions to distinguish coherent from incoherent discourse.' (W. Labov) Is this claim tenable?

4. 'In any society, and in the language of any speaker or writer, there will be errors which must be overlooked if communication is to take place.' (M. Morris) How does this relate to the integrationist view of contextualization?

5. 'One should not expect to be able to find a limited set of speech activities.' (J.J. Gumperz) Why not? And if there are an infinite number of such activities, how does this affect the possibility of constructing a satisfactory theory?

5

Language and Writing

Writing is a form of communication which occupies a unique and curious place in orthodox linguistics. Most orthodox linguistic theorists are keen to establish that writing is not language, and thus does not fall as such within the domain of linguistics. Nevertheless they acknowledge its intimate relationship to language and so accord it a privileged place among non-linguistic systems of communication. Bloomfield, for example, states quite unequivocally (Bloomfield, 1935, p.20): 'Writing is not language, but merely a way of recording language by means of visible marks.' Saussure (Saussure, 1922, p. 45) says: 'The object of study in linguistics is not a combination of the written word and the spoken word. The spoken word alone constitutes that object.' According to Nida (Nida, 1949, p.1), 'the written form of the language is entirely secondary (in fact, quite irrelevant) so far as the descriptive linguist is concerned.' Martinet (Martinet, 1964, p.17) echoes this when he writes: 'The study of writing is a discipline distinct from linguistics proper, although practically speaking it is one of its dependencies. Thus the linguist in principle operates without regard for written forms.'

For the integrationist,
(i) speech and writing cannot be separated in this way,
(ii) the equation of language with speech is untenable,
(iii) writing is not merely a way of recording the spoken word, and
(iv) the study of writing is not one of the 'dependencies' of 'linguistics proper' if 'linguistics proper' is construed as concerned solely with the study of speech.

In short, the integrationist position is opposed to the orthodox position on all possible counts with regard to the status and study of writing.

Writing and linguistics

It is important to understand in the first place why orthodox linguistics is so anxious to keep speech and writing in segregated compartments. Bloomfield lays all kinds of mistakes at the door of earlier scholars who allegedly conflated the two.

> They had not observed the sounds of speech, and confused them with the written symbols of the alphabet. This failure to distinguish between actual speech and the use of writing distorted also their notions about the history of language. They saw that in medieval and modern times highly cultivated persons wrote (and even spoke) good Latin, while less educated or careless scribes made many mistakes: failing to see that this Latin-writing was an artificial and academic exercise, they concluded that languages are preserved by the usage of educated and careful people and changed by the corruptions of the vulgar. (Bloomfield, 1935, p.8)

According to Martinet, 'everything conspires to identify in the minds of educated people the vocal sign with its graphic equivalent and to establish this latter as the sole valid representative of the complex' (Martinet, 1964, p.17).

But none of this pinpoints the basic reasons for the exclusion of writing from the domain of orthodox linguistics. There are two reasons and they are interrelated. One is that if the written word were admitted as an alternative to the spoken word as a means of linguistic expression, then literate communities would have to be treated differently for purposes of linguistic analysis from pre-literate communities. Many linguistic communities would need to be divided into two or perhaps more subcommunities, depending on the degree of literacy of the members. The linguistic knowledge of a literate person would have to be treated as being cognitively of a different order from the linguistic knowledge of a pre-literate person. All this would threaten the unity of linguistics as a discipline. It would require different techniques of analysis and different criteria of evidence in the various cases.

The second reason is closely connected with this. In practice, orthodox linguistics accepts what Saussure called the 'linearity' of the linguistic sign. Orthodox analyses of phonology, morphology and syntax are all based on the assumption that linguistic forms obey a principle of simple concatenation. One unit follows another in sequence. And this assumption works reasonably well if the linguistic form is a spoken form. But as soon as we consider written forms it no longer holds. Writing, unlike speech, cannot plausibly be treated as one-dimensional. A theory of the linguistic sign which fits speech communication cannot simply be carried over to cater for writing.

Including writing on a par with speech would require a complete revision of the theoretical basis of linguistics and a different methodology.

These are not considerations that carry any weight at all from an integrationist point of view, and for a very fundamental reason. For the integrationist, no form of communication is a self-contained activity anyway. All forms of communication necessarily involve an integration of activities. So there is no basis for treating either speech or writing as if these had arisen as independent, autonomous processes by which one individual made contact with another, just as travel by sea and travel by air offer alternative but quite unrelated ways of crossing the Atlantic to visit a friend.

For the integrationist, consequently, the first question that has to be asked about writing as a form of communication is: what activities does it integrate? By contrast, the first question an orthodox linguist asks is: what form of speech does it represent? This could hardly be the starting point for an integrationist, because for an integrationist there are forms of writing that have no connexion with speech at all. Examples of this are musical notation and mathematical notation. The integrationist proposes a theory of written communication which is far broader in its conception of what writing is than anything orthodox linguistics allows for.

Writing and speech

In twentieth-century linguistics the only orthodox school to admit the parity of writing with speech is the Copenhagen school of glossematics. It is therefore of some interest to compare the glossematic position on writing with the integrationist position.

The founder of glossematics, Louis Hjelmslev (1899-1965), held that linguistic units are independent of their expression in speech, writing, or any other material form (Siertsema, 1965, pp.111ff.). He maintained that this followed logically from accepting Saussure's dictum that a language is a form, not a substance.

> Thus the system is independent of the specific substance in which it is expressed; a given system may be equally well expressed in any one of several substances, e.g. in writing as well as in sounds.[...] The fact that articulated sound is the most common means of expression is not a consequence of any particularity inherent in the system, but is due to the anatomic-physiological constitution of man. (Siertsema, 1965, pp.111-112)

Similar views are voiced by other glossematicians. According to Uldall, for example:

it is only through the concept of a difference between form and substance that we can explain the possibility of speech and writing existing at the same time as expressions of one and the same language. If either of these substances, the stream of air or the stream of ink, were an integral part of the language itself, it would not be possible to go from one to the other without changing the language. [...] ink may be substituted for air without any change in the language [...] When we write a phonetic or a phonemic transcription we substitute ink for air, but the form remains the same, because the functions of each component form have not been changed. (Siertsema, 1965, p.113)

An initial point to note about the glossematic position on writing is that although it purports to be Saussurean, it does not correspond to the position that Saussure himself took. Saussure made it quite clear that in his terminology anything that qualified as a *langue* must be a system of articulated speech. We have a quite categorical statement in the *Cours*:

A language and its written form constitute two separate systems of signs. The sole reason for the existence of the latter is to represent the former. (Saussure, 1922, p.45)

This is difficult to reconcile with Hjelmslev's view, according to which speech takes no priority over writing at all. For Hjelmslev the language itself is an entirely abstract system, which can be manifested in *any* appropriate material form. This again is born out by Uldall, who claims:

The system of speech and the system of writing are [...] only two realizations of an infinite number of possible systems, of which no one can be said to be more fundamental than any other. (Siertsema, 1965, p.118)

This is clearly in conflict with the usual orthodox position, of which the following statement by Robins is typical:

Every natural language is primarily a spoken medium of communication, and the forms of written languages [...] are obviously controlled and are to be understood by reference to the essential spoken nature of language. (Robins, 1989, p.368)

One objection that has been raised to the glossematic position is that in fact the written language does not always correspond exactly to the spoken language: so it becomes implausible to treat both as equivalent manifestations of exactly the same underlying abstract system. There are often, for instance, words that are spelled alike but pronounced differently. Hjelmslev acknowledges that 'not all orthographies are "phonetic"' (Hjelmslev, 1961, p.104). But he claims that this is irrelevant: 'it does not alter the general fact that a linguistic form is manifested in the given substance' (Hjelmslev, 1961, p.105). He goes on to add that

> the task of the linguistic theoretician is not merely that of describing the actually present expression system, but of calculating what expression systems in general are possible as expression for a given content system, *and vice versa.* (Hjelmslev, 1961, p.105)

It seems that Hjelmslev was confusing two issues. The one on which he was right (at least, within the constraints of his own theoretical framework) was whether, in principle, it is possible for a given abstract system to have materially different but exactly equivalent manifestations, involving, for example, quite different sensory modalities. There seems no good reason to deny this, given the glossematic theoretical framework. For instance, suppose we have a waiting room in which a light flashes when it is time for the next person in the queue to go in to an inner room and be attended to. An exactly equivalent system could replace the light by a buzzer, thus substituting an auditory for a visual signal. Furthermore, there might be a significant distinction between the light flashing once and the light flashing twice. Perhaps it flashes once for the next man in the queue and twice for the next woman in the queue, because men and women are attended to separately. Again, this could be replaced by a distinction between one and two buzzes on the buzzer. And in general, for any number of such distinctions, the buzzer will do as well as the light. This would be a paradigm case to illustrate the glossematic thesis that the same abstract system can be manifested in exactly equivalent ways, although in substantially different signals.

It is worth pointing out at this juncture that for an integrationist, on the other hand, there is no equivalence between the light system and the buzzer system, because the activities integrated are not the same. They belong to biomechanically different dimensions. A blind person would not be able to respond to the light signals; nor a deaf person to the buzzer. But even in the case of individuals with normal sight and vision there is no question of integrational parity between the two systems. In order that two systems should have integrational parity it would be necessary that the activities belong to the same perceptual modalities in both cases and also that the same biomechanical abilities be exercised within those modalities. These conditions are clearly not satisfied in the case of the light and the buzzer. In other words, the glossematic position is in this respect at quite the opposite end of the theoretical spectrum from the integrationist position. In effect the glossematician simply abstracts from the actual human activities involved; whereas the integrationist places them in the forefront of the analysis.

Hjelmslev, on the other hand, is wrong, even in terms of his own theoretical framework, to deny the relevance of the fact that orthographies do not always match differences in pronunciation. He seems not to realize the force of the objection. The objection is that a single written unit may correspond to two different spoken units, as in the case of the noun *refuse* and the verb *refuse*, but this orthographic identity does not automatically obliterate any difference of meaning. All that happens in such cases is that those familiar with written English learn – to put it in traditional terms – that there are quite different usages, grammatical constructions and pronunciations associated with a single written form. However, according to Hjelmslev, the fact that some orthographies are not phonetic shows that 'different systems of expression can correspond to one and the same system of content' (Hjelmslev, 1961, p.105). The problem is that if cases like *refuse* are admitted as actual examples of this state of affairs, it becomes theoretically possible to imagine writing systems which economize on their inventory of orthographically distinct words by allowing homographs to proliferate. The *reductio ad absurdum* would be a writing system which had only one word.

Even Hjelmslev, presumably, would regard a single polysemous homograph as inadequate to manifest in ink the abstract linguistic system of English, whatever that might be. But he offers no rule to determine the limit beyond which the deployment of homographs corresponding to phonetically or semantically distinct units will introduce a non-equivalence between the spoken language and the written language.

The difficulty is compounded by Uldall, who claims:

> If we keep the units of content constant, we shall have the same language whatever system is used to make up the corresponding units of expression. [...] a system of any internal structure will do, provided that a sufficient number of units can be made up from it to express the units of content. (Siertsema, 1965, p.118)

This seems to imply that at least as many distinct units of expression are needed as there are units of content in the language. Which in turn means that any vocal or graphic systems which allow cases of homophony or homography automatically misrepresent the content system of the language. But that in turn leads to the paradoxical conclusion that neither English speech nor English writing properly express English. It is paradoxical because without English speech or English writing it is difficult to see what kind of existence the English language would have. Furthermore, if it is possible in principle that speech and writing may misrepresent the structure of a language, there seems to be no *a priori* reason to assume that we can with any assurance detect which elements of phonic or graphic manifestation correctly represent the structure of the language and which, on the other hand, do not.

In brief, glossematics shows us what happens in linguistics when the doctrine of the fixed code is idealized to the point where it is assumed to exist independently of any specific materialization whatsoever. It is clear, therefore, that whatever similarity there may at first sight seem to be between the integrationist position on writing and the glossematic position is entirely superficial. Theoretically, the two approaches could hardly be further apart.

Writing as integration

Let us now return to the question of what activities are integrated by writing as a form of communication. The first point to note is that these activities are on the whole much more varied than in the case of speech, which is another reason why they pose problems for the orthodox linguistic framework. Biomechanically, speech deploys only one mode of production; namely, vocal articulation. Writing deploys many. Writing with pen and ink, for example, is already an accomplishment involving the use of tools and programmes of motor co-ordination that are far more complex than in the case of spoken utterances. But writing with pen and ink is in turn a biomechanically different activity from using a typewriter. For particular individuals, it may be possible to write in one way but not in the other. No such division of skills arises in the case of speech: or, at least, did not until very recently when modern technology made machine-assisted speech available to individuals who would not otherwise be able to speak at all.

Just as, in speech, sounds are uttered in order to be heard, so, in writing, written forms are produced in order to be read. Here we come to further activities that the communication process integrates. But just as the production of writing can take various biomechanical forms, so can reading. This is a point which has caused much confusion among theorists. The usual assumption is that reading involves some form of optical scanning of a text, and consequently the written sign is automatically treated as a visual sign by definition. From an integrationist point of view this is a mistake. It is quite true that most people read by sight. But this is not biomechanically necessary. The discovery that the blind are able to read by touch is usually credited to Valentin Haüy, who founded the National Institute for Blind Children in Paris. It was his pupil, Louis Braille, who devised the system now known as braille writing.

This was a discovery of first-class importance for the theory of writing, although most theorists failed to realize it and carried on assuming that written signs are by definition visual, just as spoken signs are by definition auditory. It was important for two reasons. First, there is no *a priori* reason to assume that a blind person will be able to read by touch. This was the genuine discovery of a biomechanical fact, just as the discovery of the circulation of the blood was the discovery of a biomechanical fact. Second, what that discovery shows is that the form of organization on which writing depends is not visual but spatial. Vision is only a means of accessing spatial information.

This has very important implications from an integrational point of view. Briefly, it means that the basic parameters for an analysis of written forms have to be spatial. They have nothing to do with speech, which is organized in term of distinctions that are quite independent of space, except in a purely external way; i.e. inasmuch as the physical location of speaker and hearer are relevant to the viability of speech communication between them and sometimes to the message as well. However, the internal analysis of a given utterance has a temporal dimension but no spatial dimension.

It might seem initially that recognizing the spatial dimension of writing raises an insurmountable barrier between writing and speech, and thus in some sense merely confirms the view adopted in orthodox linguistics that they must be kept separate. But this is far from being the case because, as the integrationist will be quick to point out, one of the human activities subject to integration in the process of writing is speech itself. When we read a text aloud, that is precisely what we are doing: integrating two biomechanically different forms of activity. The process is so familiar that we fail to notice that our ability to do it illustrates another biomechanical fact that can hardly be taken for granted. The human brain might have been organized in a way that made reading aloud impossible or extremely difficult because of the lack of connexions between the visual processing mechanisms and those that control vocalization. Had this been so, then all reading would have had to be what we now call 'silent reading'. Thus the whole function of writing in society would have been different. The whole history of music would probably have been different too, because of the impracticality of singing at sight from a score.

The general point to be stressed here is that, unlike orthodox linguistics, the integrational approach, because it takes into consideration the biomechanical foundations of writing, enables us to do two things. One is to construct a general typology of writing in which classifications can be made according to the activities integrated. The other, which is a by-product of this, is to see exactly how speech and writing are related. Writing in the sense in which orthodox linguists refer to writing occupies only one subdivision of the whole. It comprises what integrationists call **glottic** writing: that is to say, forms of writing that are specifically designed to be integrated with speech communication. The enormous importance that is attributed to glottic writing has to do with its widespread use in administration, education and other forms of social organization. But this should not blind us to the fact that, in theoretical terms, that does not give it any privileged position. On the contrary, if we make the mistake of assuming, as orthdox linguistics does, that glottic writing is the paradigm case, and furthermore that its essential function is to *represent* different forms of speech, rather than to *integrate* speech with other activities, then we shall end up with an entirely distorted picture of *Homo scribens.*

The writing process

Given a set of activities to be integrated through writing, the integrationist distinguishes three phases in this process. But these are not phases which are to be envisaged as separate stages through which 'the message' has to be passed, as if it were an object being sent along a conveyor belt in a factory and having something different done to it at various points along the way.

With that important proviso in mind, let us call the first phase **forming**. If I want to write a letter to someone, and I have a sheet of paper and a pen or pencil, I will proceed to make visible marks in a more or less systematic way on one or both surfaces of the paper. When I have done that, or as much of it as I need to do for purposes of that particular letter, the forming phase is complete. And that phase essentially involves imposing a new organization upon what was originally a blank space. The result is a new spatial configuration for which the surface of the paper acts both as a material support and also as a frame. There is a great deal more to be said about this configuration and how it is put in place; but for the moment we are concerned simply with identifying the principal phases in the general process of written communication. The main point here is that forming does not necessarily have to be a phase which involves scoring a surface or leaving traces upon it. It might, for example, involve arranging a free-standing set of objects, or showing a pattern of coloured lights. All that is technically required is organizing or re-organizing some set of spatial relations. This much writing has in common with drawing, painting, sculpture, ceramics, and many other art forms.

The end-product of the forming phase then goes through a second phase, which we may call **processing**. Processing is what my correspondent has to engage in when my letter arrives – always assuming that my correspondent decides to read what I have written rather than throwing it straight in the waste-paper bin. The kind of processing required in that particular case is optical scanning. But again it is important to bear in mind that optical scanning is only one possible form of processing. A blind person reading a text in braille will engage in tactile processing. Processing includes any activity or sequence of activities by means of which what is written is examined for purposes of interpretation.

Interpretation is the third and final phase of written communication. In interpretation the reader engages in some further complementary activity as a result of the processing. Exactly what that is will again depend on the case. The pitfall that needs to be avoided here is to suppose that interpretation necessarily involves the kind of mental operation that is usually called 'understanding' what is written (which, according to the currently fashionable orthodoxy, means translating it into a cerebral language called 'mentalese'). This assumption, it should be noted, is an inevitable corollary of the orthodox doctrine of telementation, which construes communication as a process of thought-transference between one mind and another. This is not what an integrationist means by *interpretation*. It is possible to interpret a glottic text even if you have no idea of what language it might be written in or have no idea of whether it is a glottic text or not. I could do that, for example, if presented with a text consisting of a sequence of symbols of the International Phonetic Alphabet, and my interpretation would consist simply of reading the text aloud. In the case of reading a musical score, interpretation consists typically of producing sounds on a musical instrument.

To clarify this point, it is worth noting that in everyday usage the word *interpret* often seems to imply that you can interpret a text without necessarily doing anything about the message. So doing something about it (for instance, complying with an instruction) would then count as something extra to the interpretation. A musician could in this sense interpret the score mentally without actually playing any notes on the piano. The trouble with this from an integrational point of view is that it puts the cart before the horse. To be sure, the musician does not necessarily have to sit down at the piano and start playing. The actual execution can be withheld But nevertheless it is that further activity which has to be integrated, if only in anticipation, before the score has been interpreted in the integrationist's sense. The musician has to know what would count as playing the music, even if there happens to be no instrument handy. A musical score does not make any sense at all unless the ultimate activity to be integrated is its execution.

Someone might perhaps object that it is possible to write a musical score that is unplayable. It is also possible more generally to give written instructions that cannot be carried out. But that does not affect the theoretical point that instructions would not be instructions at all unless they envisaged some course of action required for compliance with them. It is the integration of this course of action, whatever it may be, that is envisaged in the written message. Communication, for the integrationist, essentially involves the anticipated integration of certain forms of activity. That the sequence may in practice be interrupted or abandoned before running its full course is irrelevant to the theoretical analysis. Just as the fact that games of cricket are often interrupted or abandoned because of rain does not in any way affect our understanding of how cricket is played.

Writing is not the only form of communication that can be analysed in terms of the three phases of forming, processing and interpretation. Nor is this surprising, since the analysis is derived from the more basic principle of cotemporality, which treats all human communication as designed to integrate past, present and future activities. But writing has some special features which are not characteristic of other forms of communication. For instance, if I wish to greet my friend Paul whom I see on the other side of the street, I could cross the road and say 'Hello!'. But I could stay on my side of the street and give him an affable wave of the hand. This would be an example of gestural communication. The forming phase is constituted by the wave that I execute with my hand and arm. The processing phase is constituted by my acquaintance's visual appraisal of this performance. He has to satisfy himself about the physiology and dynamics of this gesture. I might, after all, be waving my fist at him or making some vulgar insult. I might even be waving to someone else. The interpretation which I anticipate is some acknowledgment of my greeting. He might wave back. He might give me a nod, or a smile. He might even cross the road to have a word with me. If he pointedly ignores me and walks straight on as if nothing had happened, that is also an interpretational response, although not presumably what I had hoped for. If we compare this activity sequence with the corresponding sequence in the case of my writing a letter, we can note an interesting appendage of the forming phase in writing.

I, the writer, deploy in writing some of the same biomechanical techniques that my correspondent will deploy in processing the message. Typically, I will scan the letter before sending it, thereby anticipating the activity my correspondent will engage in on receiving it. I adopt the role of reader myself before requiring anyone else to adopt that role. Not so in the case of waving to my acquaintance on the other side of the street. I do not stand back and try to watch myself waving in order to make sure that I am doing it appropriately. Nor do I mentally rehearse the processing procedure that I assume he will engage in when he sees me waving. Doubtless I could, but typically I do not. Whereas typically I *do* scan the words I write, even if I could write them down without bothering to look at the paper.

I may even, in the case of writing a letter, put it aside and scan it again later and perhaps make alterations before actually sending it. So the whole 'forming' phase may be quite prolonged and have an internal pattern of its own, with recurrent loops of inscribing and scanning. What this illustrates is that by approaching communication from an integrational point of view our attention is drawn to features that will enable us to compare different forms of communication in terms of the sequential structures that are typically involved.

Writing and space

Now let us focus on what is central, according to the integrationist account, in the whole enterprise of writing: namely, the spatial configuration that is the product of the forming phase. This is largely ignored by the orthodox linguistic account, except for one feature. It is assumed that the spatial arrangement of written marks will be ordered in such a way as to correspond to the temporal ordering of a corresponding spoken utterance. And this is based on the prior orthodox assumption that writing exists merely in order to represent speech. Saussure even says at one point in his discussion of linguistic signs that their linearity is immediately apparent when they are represented in writing: 'a spatial line of graphic signs is substituted for a succession of sounds in time' (Saussure, 1922, p.103).

This is a quite astonishing pronouncement and repays examination. In the first place, the temporal properties of sound sequences in a spoken utterance are not those of a line. The concept of a line is a spatial concept. There are no lines in time. There are none in speech. A line can turn back upon itself, loop round and join up with itself at its starting point. Speech can do none of these things. A line always extends in two directions. You can follow it from X to Y or from Y to X. Or you can start in the middle and follow it in either direction. Speech has only one 'direction'. If speech is mapped physically on to a linear structure, as it is in a tape recording, the first thing that you discover if you play the tape backwards is that the speech becomes quite unrecognizable. And there is no vocal performance that human beings can manage which corresponds to reversing the tape.

For all these reasons, it is impossible to regard the claim that speech is linear as anything other than a metaphor. But it is a very misleading metaphor on several counts. The sense in which, say, writing in the Roman alphabet is linear requires us to distinguish various kinds or levels of linearity, all of of which may be relevant to the processing phase in the case of written texts, but none of which applies to speech. First, the writing is linear in that each character in the Roman alphabet can take the form of a continuous linear mark on a surface. The only exception to this is the lower case roman i, and the exception is only apparent. That is to say, the dot over the i is historically an added diacritic, introduced in order to distinguish it from other letters. Second, the writing can be linear in the sense that a single uninterrupted line can join up sequences of letters into larger units. This happens in some forms of handwriting but not typically in print, where the separate characters are discrete. Third, alphabetic texts are usually written in such a way that the processing phase requires scanning that follows an imaginary line that proceeds horizontally from side to side of the page, but without intersecting itself. This is presumably what Saussure had in mind when he referred to 'the spatial line of graphic signs'.

It is obvious, however, that this does not correspond to the processing requirements for speech. Auditorily, we cannot track the sound sequence backwards even if we wanted to, and there is no sense in which we could track from side to side. But a more important point is that the supposed parallel between the organization of speech and the organization of writing overlooks a fundamental difference. That is: the sequentiality of sound is imposed upon us by a biomechanical constraint. It has to do with the physiology of the vocal apparatus. The sequence of written characters is not imposed on us by any such constraint: it is a feature of particular writing systems, not of writing as such. It would be perfectly possible to devise a form of writing, even using the Roman alphabet, in which the processing order was not linear in this third sense. In other words, we could devise a system in which the order was indicated by some other means than relative position on the surface; for example, by relative size. This might not be as convenient for rapid optical processing as the systems we have, but there is nothing inherently impossible about it.

Defining writing

Writing as a form of communication shares many features with drawing, painting and others which typically involve the marking of surfaces and the organization of spatial relations. The question is: what distinguishes writing from these neighbouring forms of communication? This question has to be answered by any theorist who claims to be offering a theory of writing. But it is surprising how often this requirement is overlooked. For instance, I.J. Gelb, one of the leading authorities on the history of writing during the latter half of the twentieth century, offered the following definition of writing: 'a system of human intercommunication by means of conventional visible marks' (Gelb, 1963, p.v). Although this does not fall into the orthodox linguist's error of defining writing by reference to speech, it errs at the other extreme by being far too broad. Perspective drawing, as developed by Alberti and his followers, qualifies as a system of human communication by means of conventional visible marks. But it hardly counts as writing, unless indeed that term is extended to include picture-making.

The question is complicated by the fact that, according to traditional wisdom, writing began as a simplified form of pictorial drawing. The evidence for this theory is questionable, to say the least. But the popularity of the theory explains in part why some authorities find it attractive to adopt the orthodox linguistic position and define writing by reference to speech. It then becomes possible to claim that 'real' writing began when the pictures changed from being representations of things to being representations of words. We need not pursue here the difficulties that this account runs into. However, the integrationist definition of writing has an altogether different basis, which is as follows.

What is needed is a set of criteria that distinguish writing on the one hand from gesture and on the other hand from drawing. The distinction between writing and gesture is needed because the integrationist does not define writing in terms of marks on a surface. Even though many forms of writing do in practice involve marking a surface, that is not a necessary condition. For instance, sky-writing as practised by commercial advertising agents, does not require a surface. The writing is formed by means of an airborne apparatus which controls the emission of a stream of smoke into the atmosphere. Neon lighting is another means of producing written signs without the use of a surface.

On the other hand, the organization of spatial relations will not suffice to distinguish writing from gesture because, as for instance in the sign languages of the deaf, the relevant gestures are also spatially organized. It may be noted in passing that the problem cannot be solved by the strategy adopted in orthodox linguistics, because if the representation of speech is taken as criterial that too can be accomplished by means of a gestural system. The integrationist solution is based on the same general principle that motivates all integrational distinctions; namely, that communication depends on the activities integrated. And here the relevant consideration is *the processing phase.* If written signs vanished as quickly as they were produced, then there would indeed be no difference between writing and gesture. What is characteristic of writing is that the forms have a temporal duration which allows for reprocessing; which in the case of visual processing involves multiple scanning. In that sense, writing is static, whereas gesture is kinetic. The possibility of reprocessing is extremely important for social and cognitive reasons. It allows written information to be checked. That is precisely why documents have played such an important part in the development of civilization. In kinetic forms of communication, on the other hand, there is no possibility of reprocessing unless the original sign or series of signs is repeated. That is also true of speech, which is likewise ephemeral. Even the use of a recording machine does not make speech reprocessable unless the auditory signal is replayed. Once again, the principle of cotemporality holds the key to an integrational analysis of communication.

The integrational way of distinguishing writing from drawing also appeals to the processing phase of communication, but in a different manner. What characterizes writing is that you have to process the signs in a specific order, not at random. In other words, the spatial organization of the written text has to be such that the right order of signs is retrievable. That is the basic reason why so often writing is organized in rows or columns. That is not a requirement in the case of drawing. You can scan a typical drawing in any order you care to, or in various orders on separate occasions: it will in the end make no difference to your assessment of the visual information the drawing presents. In brief, writing operates on the basis of a pre-arranged processing pattern: drawing does not. Drawing allows free processing, which in visual terms means free optical scanning.

Thus all the basic requirements for a theory of writing can be met by adopting an integrational approach. It does not require us to define writing by reference to speech; but at the same time it can accommodate and explain exactly how writing and speech function as integrated activities.

Writing and codification

Glottic writing is also important to the integrationist for a quite different reason from any mentioned above. Writing is a tool which enables speech to be codified. Grammar books and dictionaries, as developed in Western culture, are based on writing. This has important consequences not only in that access to these codifications requires literacy, and therefore puts educational programmes on a different basis than any available in preliterate societies, but also for the development of linguistic reflexivity. In a literate society, one learns to think of speech in terms of how it might be written down, and hence to regard the written language as a kind of model for 'good' speech. The integrationist term for this kind of priority that characterizes attitudes to language in literate societies is **scriptism**.

Scriptism is important because it pervades the kind of metalanguage that develops in literate societies. Writing itself provides a new way of discussing utterances, of identifying 'what was said'. The sounds of speech come to be referred to in terms of the corresponding written characters. We see this already established in Greek metalinguistic discussion by the time of Plato's *Cratylus*, where both the sounds of a word and the corresponding alphabetic letters are designated indifferently by the term *grammata* and individual sounds are referred to by the name of the corresponding letter (*alpha*, *beta*, etc.). It would be naive to conclude from this that Plato and his contemporaries actually failed to grasp the difference between sounds and letters, but their metalinguistic practice indicates very clearly the extent to which they already thought of speech as an oral counterpart of writing rather than of writing as a visual counterpart of speech.

Alphabetic writing provides in itself a codification of spoken communication at a very elementary level. It is, to use the term that Renaissance and post-Renaissance scholars were fond of employing, a way of 'reducing' speech. At the same time, it provides a very powerful tool for the decontextualization and recontextualization of speech. It detaches the spoken word from the speaker and makes it 're-presentable' in another context. This possibility is an important basis for the notion of context-free forms and context-free meanings that has come to dominate not only lexicography but modern linguistics as well.

The advent of writing thus constitutes a milestone in the cultural history of any community. Once its members become literate, their notion of 'speech' will never be the same again. Writing, as Love puts it,

> achieves the object of fixing the identification of utterances (in the limited sense of providing them with something outside speech itself to which they could be referred) by simply laying down what it is your utterance was an utterance of. If you write it *CAT*, then *that* is what you said. (Love, 1998)

Not only does a preliterate society have no means of 'recording' speech, but – more importantly – it has no means of conceptualizing speech as a counterpart *of anything else*. The identification of language with speech is total and inevitable.

Further reading

- Harris and Wolf, 1998, Part 5, 'Language and Writing'
- On literacy: Ong 1982
- On writing: Harris 1996a

Questions for discussion

1. 'Developing a written counterpart to spoken language removes the difficulties attaching to a purely oral practice of metalinguistic discourse' (N. Love). What advantages and disadvantages does this bring in its wake?
2. 'Writing is the graphic counterpart of speech' (D. Diringer). What qualifications would an integrationist wish to make to this statement?
3. 'Writing is clearly an optional accessory; the real engine of verbal communication is the spoken language we acquired as children' (S. Pinker) Comment on the notions 'optional' and 'accessory' with reference to life in literate societies.
4. 'Writing began at the time when man learnt how to communicate his thoughts and meanings by means of visible signs' (I.J. Gelb). What are the limitations of thinking about writing in this way?
5. 'Writing restructures consciousness' (W.J. Ong). What aspects of this 'restructuring' would an integrationist emphasize?

6

Language and Society

Integrationists have applied integrational principles to a variety of practical linguistic questions that arise as part of everyday social intercourse, ranging from language-teaching (Davis, D.R., 1998) to translation (Morris, 1998), and from attitudes to swearing (Davis, H.G., 1998) to attitudes to how people pronounce your name (Wolf et al., 1998) . The present chapter does not attempt to summarize or comment on particular investigations of this kind, but deals with certain general questions that arise out of them. These are questions bearing on what the integrationist recognizes as the **'macrosocial'** dimension of language.

Whereas orthodox linguistics starts from an assumption about languages as fixed codes *already* common to a linguistic community, integrational linguistics proposes a different point of departure. This is recognition of the **individuality of linguistic experience**. The question that immediately arises is this. If linguistic experience inevitably differs from one individual to another, what is the relationship between *A*'s 'language', *B*'s 'language' and that communal 'language' which (let us suppose) *A* and *B* both regard themselves (and each other) as speaking.

The integrationist answer is that this will vary according to the way in which, on particular occasions, *A* and/or *B* contextualize their own discourse in relation to an abstraction which they posit as a social norm.

This answer, however, automatically raises a further question. One way of putting this question would be: 'What, then, is a linguistic fact? ' For if linguistic facts are ultimately facts about individuals acting in certain ways on particular occasions, how can there be any general study or discipline laying claim to a systematic analysis – or even identification – of such facts? And if no answer is forthcoming, is not this tantamount to declaring the whole enterprise of linguistics – or, at the very least, sociolinguistics – null and void?

Are linguistic facts social facts?

In 1975 a leading theorist of segregationism in sociolinguistics, William Labov, published a paper on linguistic theory addressed to exactly the question raised in the preceding paragraph. The paper was called 'What is a linguistic fact?'. It raises a number of issues that are very relevant to the integrationist approach.

A linguistics which postulates linguistic facts amenable to description, but then in practice cannot identify such facts with any assurance, is clearly on a hiding to nothing. This much Labov recognizes. He restricts his observations explicitly to linguistics in America, but it is difficult to imagine that he thought that his general conclusions did not have a wider application.

In this paper Labov tries to grapple with the problem of basing linguistic descriptions on the evidence afforded by introspective judgments. (This is already a recognition of the reflexivity of language, although Labov does not identify it as such.) Introspective judgments can be made either by the linguist or by the linguist's informants. (The judgments are referred to, somewhat bizarrely, as 'intuitions' of 'grammaticality': the phrase is unpardonably question-begging, but let us set that on one side for present purposes.) Labov draws attention to the disconcerting tendency among linguists to treat their own introspective judgments as 'linguistic facts', and to the copious evidence which indicates that lay informants often disagree with linguists on the key examples used by linguists to support their own analyses. As Labov shrewdly observes, conflicts of evidence often do not surface in the work of many linguists because of their willingness to treat just one or two informants as representative of a whole speech community. When inquiries are more exhaustive, however, discrepancies between speakers are readily brought to light.

It is clear that for Labov there are 'good' and 'bad' answers to the question 'What is a linguistic fact?'. The worst possible answer would be that a linguistic fact is what a linguist declares to be one, simply on the basis of personal judgment. For then the whole edifice of linguistics *qua* 'science' would collapse in ruins, and the partisans of hocus-pocus would run riot.

To avoid this desperate outcome Labov proposes a number of 'principles' to be followed in constructing linguistic descriptions. These principles are in fact recommendations or guidelines, such as excluding from consideration in controversial cases the judgments of those familiar with linguistic theory, and disregarding introspective judgments altogether in cases where they are found to be less consistent than observed linguistic behaviour. There are four principles in all, and they do not need to be considered in detail here. As far as they go, the principles are doubtless sensible; but what Labov does not seem to see is that the very need to make such recommendations highlights a far bigger problem about the status of 'linguistic facts'. And this problem is one that his recommendations leave untouched.

It is a problem that brings us back to the terms 'intuition' and 'grammaticality', as well as to the whole theoretical framework within which the sociolinguistic enterprise is situated. Grammaticality, as construed in modern linguistics, is hardly something about which it is possible to have intuitions, any more than it is possible to have intuitions about the theory of gravitation. Perhaps Newton once had such an intuition when the apple hit him on the head; but it would be odd to call our everyday expectation that objects will fall if dropped an intuition, and even more absurd to call it an intuition of the law of gravitation. What typically happens when a linguist is extracting these supposed intuitions of grammaticality from an informant is that the informant is asked to pass judgment on some decontextualized sentence or set of sentences. Exactly what the judgment is supposed to be *about* is clearly crucial to the reply; but Labov, significantly, passes over this in silence. It seems fairly obvious that a reply might differ depending on whether one were asked, for instance, whether the sentence infringes any grammatical rule, whether it makes sense, whether it conforms to current usage, whether one would say it oneself, whether one can imagine it being said, whether one regards it as 'good English', and so on. These are all different questions, and, furthermore, they are culturally loaded questions. They presuppose a culture in which 'correct' speech and writing are educational priorities and social markers. They presuppose a culture in which it makes sense in the first place to ask for metalinguistic judgments on random samples of isolated sentences divorced from any communicational function. (On societies where this is not a viable form of inquiry, see Mühlhäusler, 1982.) It would be, to say the least, optimistic to suppose that Labov's procedural recommendations for dealing with conflicting judgments somehow screened out all these issues of interpretation to yield a residue of *bona fide* 'linguistic facts'.

Nor can the problem be circumvented by trying to construct elicitation procedures that avoid confronting the informant with a direct question. For then all the difficulties just mentioned are further complicated by the overarching difficulty of demonstrating that the indirect procedures do actually supply answers to the direct questions that have been avoided.

What stands in the way of Labov's programme is that it tries to do something that is impossible; namely, reconcile the technique of the Gallup poll with the basic tenets of the language myth. This leads to the following dilemma: either *all* introspective linguistic judgments are in some way reflections of linguistic knowledge, or *none* of them are.

Hence Labov's recommended strategy of discarding or minimizing cases where one (expressed) judgment apparently contradicts another. Why do this? Because the doctrine of the fixed code demands invariant signs. Labov's adherence to this doctrine is signalled very early on in his paper, where he asserts that 'the general program of all linguists begins with the search for invariance' (Labov, 1975, p.7). Which he interprets as discovering that certain utterances are, as he puts it, 'tokens of the same type'. (For an integrationist approach to 'types' and 'tokens' in linguistic theory, see Hutton, 1990.)

Thus, for Labov, small differences in length, height or nasalization of a particular vowel may not 'make any difference in a linguistic sense'. This will depend on the word and the language in question. In such cases, says Labov, the linguist does not insist on phonetic transcriptions that record such minutiae, because they are irrelevant. In other words, the assumption is that if minor variations of pronunciation go unnoticed or are simply ignored by both speakers and hearers, they should be ignored by the linguist too. So 'omission of data and simplification of transcription is one way of stating linguistic facts' (Labov, 1975, p.8). He goes so far as to add: 'If all variation were at this superficial level, there would be no need for a linguistic analysis or for linguists'.

Social facts and psychological reality

According to Labov, then, linguists are in business only *because* getting at the 'linguistic facts' involves going beyond the perceptions of lay language-users. Nevertheless, this superior professional enterprise must somehow be made answerable to those lay perceptions. This compromise may be regarded as Labov's way of reconciling the recognition of linguistic facts as social facts with an endorsement of the Saussurean goal of 'psychological reality' in linguistic description:

> the sum total of deliberate, systematic classifications set up [...] must coincide with the sum total of associations, conscious or unconscious, operative in speech. (Saussure, 1922, p.189)

This combination yields, in Labov's hands, a methodology guided by two main principles which sit uneasily together. The first, as already mentioned, requires the linguist just to ignore 'facts' that escape the attention of the laity. Linguists need not waste their time demonstrating how much about speech escapes the attention of the *hoi polloi*. As a blend of positivism with pragmatism, this policy doubtless has a great deal to recommend it, being in obvious accord with that dictum of American folk wisdom which says: 'If it isn't broken, don't fix it.' However, if there were nothing to be fixed at all, linguists would be out of a job. This is where the second principle comes in. What the linguist can legitimately seek to do is establish the linguistic 'facts' that members of the community seem to agree on. Labov claims that whenever there is consensus on what is the same and what is different, then 'we can feel safe in assuming that we are studying *langue* as the common property of the speech community' (Labov, 1975, p.9).

This raises two problems. One is that if the consensus is already clear to lay members of the community, linguists will merely be telling them what they already know; which hardly seems a sufficient academic goal for the establishment of a whole discipline devoted to it. But if on the other hand linguists claim to have found a consensus that speakers were *not* aware of, this arguably puts a question mark against the notion of 'psychological reality' as a requirement of linguistic description.

The other problem is what happens when investigation reveals a lack of consensus. In such cases the language myth allows only two escape routes. One is to postulate that the fixed code includes items that are 'in free variation', as it is called. The other is to postulate that the 'data' collected must be a mixture pertaining to more than one fixed code. Or, as it is usually put, there must be more than one 'dialect' involved. Since additional fixed codes can be postulated *ad infinitum*, hypothetical multiplication of dialects ensures that we can always, as Labov expresses it, 'fit the object of our description to the consistency of the data' (Labov, 1975, p.12).

Labov sees that there is something questionable about this manœuvre and seeks to restrict its deployment. But the rigidity of his theoretical framework does not allow him to go as far as the integrationist position; that is, to question the fixed-code doctrine itself. Nor, on the other hand, does he find himself attracted to the other option canvassed by some linguists (see Ch.3) which is to set up a new theoretical object called the *idiolect*. This in practice, as he observes, narrows the scope of analysis to 'the speech of one person talking about one topic for a short time'. In other words, the idiolect is what the fixed-code doctrine produces when the fixed code is freed from its social moorings and attached to a single individual and a limited range of utterances by that individual. When this point is reached, clearly, the fixed code is no longer a communal (i.e. social) system, and the study of speech has been divorced from the study of communication. But what has been secured (provided the individual's speech is internally consistent) is the linguist's desired sets of invariants.

So in the end the search for invariants takes priority over everything else. Labov's preference is for one way of finding them: the description of idiolects is another. But in both cases it becomes clear that the invariants are 'manufactured' rather than 'found', and they are manufactured by imposing restrictions that are designed precisely for that purpose.

Linguistic variation revisited

Now it might be argued that there is nothing objectionable about defining 'linguistic facts' in this way provided it is all done 'above board'. But the question the integrationist asks is: what is the point of doing it at all? For what it produces is a totally artificial analysis of how, as social beings, we engage in speech communication. For example, whatever methods the linguist opts for in the search for invariants, the result is a concept of 'dialects' which is simply an artifact of those methods. It does not correspond to or illuminate the lay understanding of what is 'dialectal' in the least.

Dialect speech, in the lay sense, is recognized by the detection of features which are taken – whether rightly or wrongly makes no difference – to indicate the regional provenance of the speaker. More broadly, recognition of dialect features belongs with a continuum of other linguistic abilities pertaining to speech variation, including, for example, the detection of a foreign accent. These are what the integrationist calls 'macrosocial' phenomena. Their role in speech communication is at present poorly understood, as are the differences between individuals in sensitivity to them. But this is so in large part because orthodox linguistics, with its obsessive search for invariants, dismisses such questions from the domain of linguistics proper and relegates their investigation to psychology and sociology.

These disciplines in turn are interested in them only insofar as they are amenable to the techniques of inquiry and 'data collection' already approved for use in the investigation of non-linguistic matters. Consequently macrosocial linguistic phenomena are discussed almost entirely in terms of statistics and graphs relating to age, sex, income and other parameters dear to designers of questionnaires, and/or on the basis of tests carried out in interviews or laboratory sessions. It is open to question, for obvious reasons, whether all this tells us a great deal about what goes on in everyday communication situations; and even more so whether these modes of 'observation' do not implicitly reduce speech to the level of just another aspect of personal or social behaviour (cf. hair styles, clothes, purchase of consumer goods, eating habits, etc.) Of course, speech *is* a facet of individual and social behaviour: the integrationist does not wish to deny this. But the question is whether these forms of inquiry and documentation capture what is unique about speech and justifies setting up linguistics as an independent academic subject.

In brief, the situation boils down to this. Either – as in orthodox linguistics – the treatment of evidence is oriented towards a search for invariants; or else, as in much psychological and sociological work, speech is treated as one variable – among others – in personal or communal patterns of behaviour. There is nothing in between. And this lacuna emerges because there has been hitherto no theoretical perspective which assigns to language its primary role in human affairs. Making that assignment is the basis of integrational linguistics; and integrational linguistics stands or falls by the validity of its claim concerning that role.

A new start

Bloomfield once wrote (Bloomfield, 1935, p.21): 'Again and again, scholarship has approached the study of language without actually entering upon it.' The remark loses none of its perspicacity when we realize that Bloomfield thought that *his* generation had at last entered into that Elysium; whereas in retrospect we may doubt whether that was the case. The point at which Bloomfield and his generation lost their way was in pinning the study of language to the possibility of identifying invariants in linguistic behaviour. That, it might be urged, was a necessary precondition for the claim that linguistics is a science. All genuine sciences – the argument goes – deal with invariants: otherwise there would be no basis for the testing and verification of hypotheses. This requires that the same phenomena can be replicated in the same conditions not only once or twice but as many times, over and over again, as may be necessary. Therefore, if speech is to be the subject-matter of a science, it must be treated on the assumption, or in such a way, as to make that possible in principle. Hence the adoption of the fixed-code doctrine which, in a sense, assures us – or reassures us – of this permanent, continuing possibility in the field of language. Everything that the orthodox linguist studies *qua* linguist, in other words, has to be reducible to the recurrence of invariants. And where that is not possible, there the boundaries of linguistics are drawn. Saussure does not say this in so many words, but it is implicit in his treatment of a whole range of topics. Speech events are unrepeatable (even with technological aids such as gramophones or tape recorders); but what *can* be reiterated, again and again, are the linguistic signs that speech instantiates.

Now the permanent possibility of that reiteration requires that the linguistic sign be determinate both in form and in meaning. And this is where the integrationist joins battle with the theorists of orthodox linguistics. 'The indeterminacy of the linguistic sign is the central doctrine of integrationism' (Harris, 1998b). If that means that linguistics can no longer claim to be a science, then so be it. The way we think about language is too important for an integrationist to worry very much about whether linguistics counts as a 'science' or not. On the contrary, worrying about the 'scientific' status of linguistics is, arguably, what has most retarded the development of the subject in the present century (Harris, 1992).

Linguistic communities and linguistic determinacy

Clear thinking about language and society is impeded all too frequently by attempts to project onto the community a linguistic determinacy of the theorist's own invention. There are three common misconceptions of determinacy, which may be called (i) the 'definitional' misconception, (ii) the 'common core' misconception and (iii) the 'compulsory option' misconception (Harris, 1998b).

Linguists who fall for the first of these think that somehow the determinacy of linguistic structure is demonstrated by their ability to propose rules and categories that will cover all cases. To take a simple example, Quirk, Greenbaum, Leech and Svartvik in their *Grammar of Contemporary English* (Quirk et al., 1972, p.137) tell us that there is a rule governing English determiners which prevents more than one occurring before the head noun. This supposedly explains the ungrammaticality of phrases like *a the boy* and *a some boy*. They appear to have overlooked the existence of a determiner like *such*, which occurs in phrases like *such a boy* and *some such boy*, although elsewhere (Quirk et al., 1972, p.926) they do count *such* as a determiner. Now this problem admits two possible solutions. Either the definition of the category 'determiner' has to be redefined so as to exclude *such*, or else the rule has to be redefined so that it applies only to one subclass of determiners. Whichever option the linguist goes for will bring the recalcitrant *such* back into line as having a determinate place in the structure of English. However, it is obvious that this face-saving manœuvre can be deployed *ad infinitum* to accommodate as many 'exceptions' as you like. What has to be ensured is simply that the definitions of the rules and the definitions of the categories to which the rules apply are mutually consistent. The mistake is to suppose that the possibility of engineering this consistency is what shows the structure of English to be determinate. Why is this a mistake? Because the structure could hardly be other than determinate if *that* is the criterion. In other words, not only English but any set of random items whatsover will exhibit a determinate structure if the challenge is simply to set up a mutually consistent set of rules and categories in terms of which to describe them. The concept of determinacy becomes vacuous because there is nothing to which it is opposed. Given the availability of an unlimited number of rules and categories to define as required, indeterminacy is simply not a theoretical possibility. So any society could, on this basis, have a system of linguistic rules constructed for it.

Theorists who see what is wrong with the 'definitional' misconception of linguistic determinacy often plump for the 'common core' misconception instead. An example is Lyons, who discusses the issue of determinacy of grammatical structure in his *Introduction to Theoretical Linguistics* (Lyons, 1968, pp.152-4). Lyons holds that the grammar of English is up to a point determinate, but beyond that point indeterminate. What determines this point? According to Lyons it is determined by the consensus of speakers of English. When the English of different native speakers starts to diverge, i.e. to conform to different rules, the linguist will know that these divergences indicate that there is no longer a common core of usage underlying it.

This solution, clearly, is a variant version of Labov's. In other words, determinacy is saved by treating a mixture of dialects as responsible for the conflicting evidence. As noted earlier, what this amounts to in practice is that conflicting macrosocial evidence can always be discarded. Thus the determinacy is imposed by the linguist on the linguist's own terms: it is far from being an intrinsic feature of the describienda. Again, the solution is specious, since any form of social behaviour can be made to appear determinate by applying this strategy.

The 'compulsory option' misconception is different again. Suppose the linguist finds a community in which some processes of word-formation are widely used, but there is no consensus as to limits to which they can be taken. For instance, consider in English the formation of adjectives from nouns by adding the suffix *-less*. Examples are *speechless, childless, harmless, restless, careless, stateless, homeless, toothless*. The suffix *-less* in these cases is usually understood as meaning 'without' or 'lacking in'. So in principle there seems no reason why it might not be extended to any appropriate noun. Nevertheless, while many English speakers will happily use *carless* to describe being without a *car* fewer would use *petrolless* to describe being without *petrol* and perhaps none would spontaneously use *governmentless* to describe being without a *government*. It might seem that there is no 'rule' as to which nouns can take this particular suffix; and *pro tanto* the structure of the language is on this point indeterminate.

Linguists committed to the 'common core' misconception would deal with such cases by attempting to show that there is a set of formations ending in *-less* which all speakers agree are used, and simply discard the rest. But there is an alternative, which is to postulate a 'rule' which requires each speaker to choose whether or not the form is usable. This, clearly, corresponds to Labov's 'free variation' strategy. In this way, the language retains determinacy of structure and the apparent indeterminacy is attributed to the varying choices of individual speakers following the same determinate 'rule'.

These three misconceptions of determinacy are widespread in orthodox linguistics and often complement one another. In the first type of case, the misconception consists in identifying determinacy with the possibility of postulating categories and rules that are comprehensive, exceptionless and internally consistent. In the second type of case, determinacy is confused with uniformity of practice. In the third, determinacy is confused with fixing the limits within which individuals may exercise a linguistic choice.

Society and the 'limits' of language

None of these misconceptions of linguistic determinacy should be conflated with that sometimes invoked by logicians. Carnap, for example (Carnap, 1956), treats sentences as '*L*-determinate' if their truth-value is determined by the semantic rules of the language *L*. The symbolic languages with which Carnap and other logicians are primarily concerned are, however, fixed codes in the integrationist's sense. Traditional Western logic in general requires no less stringent guarantees of invariance than orthodox linguistics posits for languages, since otherwise there could be no systematization of syllogistic reasoning. It is somewhat paradoxical that the whole enterprise of modern symbolic logic is based on the assumption that these guarantees are lacking in the case of 'everyday' languages like English. Hence the motivation for constructing artificial notations for which such guarantees can supposedly be put in place.

More generally, philosophers of science have often assumed that fixed codes are an essential pre-requisite for any genuine 'language of science'. Hempel (1952), for instance, argues explicitly that languages like English are inadequate for science, because in the English-speaking community it is not even possible to determine what an everyday word like *hat* means. The assumption that 'we all know' what *hat* means, according to Hempel, turns out to be untenable. The conditions that would have to be satisfied cannot be satisfied. Why not? For the following reason :

> to ascertain the meaning of the word 'hat' in contemporary English as spoken in the United States, we would have to determine to what kinds of objects – no matter whether they actually occur or not – the word 'hat' would be applied according to contemporary American usage. In this sense the conception of an analysis of "the" meaning of a given expression presupposes that the conditions of its application are (1) well determined for every user of the language and are (2) the same for all users during the period of time under consideration. We shall refer to these two presuppositions as the conditions of *determinacy* and of (personal and interpersonal) *uniformity of usage*. Clearly, neither of them is fully satisfied by any natural language. (Hempel, 1952, pp.9-10)

Before proceeding to consider why Hempel thinks these conditions cannot be satisfied, it is worth noting (i) that the conditions cited correspond exactly to those postulated in what integrationists call 'the language myth', and (ii) how closely Hempel's conditions echo the worries of Labov about the identification of 'linguistic facts'. Unlike Labov, however, Hempel does not think that the problem can be finessed by choosing to pay no attention to inconvenient evidence. This is clear from what Hempel goes on to say:

> the term 'hat' is vague; i.e., various kinds of objects can be described or actually produced in regard to which one would be undecided whether to apply the term or not. In addition, the usage of the term exhibits certain inconsistencies both among different users and even for the same user of contemporary American English; i.e., instances can be described or actually produced of such a kind that different users, or even the same user at different times, will pass different judgments as to whether the term applies to those instances. (Hempel, 1952, p.10)

We may note in passing that this last remark corroborates Labov's worries about the validity of postulating 'idiolects'. An integrationist would press this point even further. The question is not simply whether I *do*, as a speaker of English, consistently apply the term *hat* over a given period of time. The condition could be met trivially by choosing a period of time during which I used the word only once. (That would be the ultimate *reductio ad absurdum* of the concept of an 'idiolect'.) The question is whether, even if I *do* use the term consistently and on many occasions over some selected period, there is any reason why I have to.

The general answer to that has to be 'no'. That is to say, there is no overriding reason why it might not suit my communicational purposes to use the term *hat* in one way in certain circumstances, but in another way in other circumstances. For instance, I might call a turban a 'hat' in some circumstances, but not in others. So my answer to the question 'Do Sikhs wear hats?' might vary according to whether I thought it would be more misleading to reply affirmatively or negatively, or whether I wanted or did not want, for whatever reason, to have Sikhs included among the hat-wearing peoples of the world. Or whether I thought I might offend a Sikh who happened to be present.

However, to return to Hempel: the reasons why he says that in actual usage the word *hat* is 'vague', i.e. not a determinate linguistic sign, are precisely the reasons an integrationist would give for saying that it cannot belong to a fixed code at all. And if this is true of an everyday term like *hat*, it poses a serious problem for orthodox linguistics. The difficulty has escaped attention because it has simply been taken for granted that somehow there must be fixed codes to which words like *hat* belong. The problem is this. If the languages we call *English, French, Latin*, etc. contain a mixture of determinate and indeterminate signs, then the first task of the linguist must be to sort out which is which. For presumably the telementational account of communication can survive only on condition that the determinate signs have some kind of priority, and the indeterminate signs are accorded a marginal role.

Thus it might conceivably be, for instance, that although *A* and *B* believe they speak 'the same language', the fact is that any given sentence *S* is likely to contain a mixture of determinate and indeterminate signs. That might account for why, although *B* understands a certain amount of what *A* says, nevertheless there are some points on which *A* may not quite succeed in communicating the desired message.

Manifestly, if this were the case for languages generally, it would be a top priority for linguistics to devise a way of identifying these two basic classes of sign. This would be much more important than arguing about how many parts of speech there are or how many phonemes in the language.

Deixis as contextual (in)determinacy

The most plausible move that modern linguistics has made in this direction is to resurrect a distinction from traditional Western grammar. This is the distinction between deictic and non-deictic expressions. Supposedly, it works in roughly the following way. Deictic expressions are words like *this, that, here, there, me, you, now, then, today* and *yesterday.* Non-deictic expressions are words like *cat, dog, run, walk, red, green, London* and *Edinburgh.* The difference is supposed to reside in the fact that deictic expressions direct attention to the context of utterance, whereas non-deictic expressions direct attention to permanent, context-free meanings. Hence grammatical features such as tense distinctions are regarded as inherently deictic. A current dictionary of linguistic terminology (Crystal, 1991, p.96) defines *deixis* as a term covering 'those features of language which refer directly to the personal, temporal or locational characteristics of the situation within which an utterance takes place, whose meaning is thus relative to that situation.'

On this view, then, a form like *went* combines both a deictic and a non-deictic element. Its use has to be understood both by reference to the non-deictic verb *go* and by reference to the deictic notion of past time relative to the moment of utterance. So we do not understand what people mean when they use the form *went* unless we grasp two quite distinct things: (i) on the one hand, the general notion of 'going', which is not tied to any particular time or place, and (ii) the idea that this form relates a particular action of going to some time prior to the utterance itself. If we do not understand both those notions, then we do not fully understand what the form *went* means. Similarly, we do not understand what is meant by the English pronoun *me* unless we grasp on the one hand the general idea of a person as an agent and can relate that to the notion that the person in question is the one doing the speaking or writing of the word *me*.

Some such account of deixis is still common coin in orthodox linguistics, and it does not differ greatly from the traditional account offered for centuries by Western grammarians. One does not have to ponder very long on this account before realizing that there is something suspect about it. According to the definition cited above, deictic devices are those which 'refer directly to the personal, temporal or locational characteristics of the situation within which an utterance takes place'. But actually that is far from being the case. On the contrary, every deictic device or expression leaves open the question of exactly who, what or when is being referred to. It is the hearer or reader who has to work that out. We see this as soon as we contrast expressions like *today* and *tomorrow* and *the day after* with expressions like *January 1st 1998, January 2nd 1998*, etc. If we had a choice between a calendar based on expressions of the former type and a calendar based on expressions of the latter type, there is little doubt which we should find most useful in recording or planning our appointments. By the same token, if we try to replace as many non-deictic expressions as possible by corresponding deictics in a newspaper headline and still cover all the possibilities we shall find that we turn an item of information into a conundrum. *Tony Blair rejects U.S. proposals for meeting in Washington* becomes *He won't have theirs (or ours) for having it there (or here).*

Now it is evident that the distinction between deictic and non-deictic expressions will not cope with Hempel's problem about indeterminacy, since by his criteria both deictics and non-deictics would be equally indeterminate, although in different ways. A non-deictic like *hat* would be no less indeterminate than a deictic like *he*. The difference would be that the indeterminacy of *he* is bound up with local problems of identifying who the speaker is talking about.

But in any case there are at least two general reasons for rejecting the orthodox account of deixis. One is that this account stands the relationship between deixis and circumstantial factors on its head. In general, the deictic expression will fit a wider range of circumstances than the non-deictic expression, precisely because there is *no* 'direct reference' to situational features or specific actors. The reason why *I love you* is a formula that will do for so many different occasions and relationships is that it fails to identify who the *I* and the *you* are. But in this respect it is no different from *Happy Christmas!* – which is also a formula that fails to specify whose seasonal greetings are conveyed to whom.

Now this relates to, but must not be conflated with, a second reason for rejecting the orthodox account. For the integrationist, this second reason is the more fundamental of the two. The orthodox account misrepresents the distinction between deictic and non-deictic devices *in any case* by treating it as a difference between context-free and context-bound meanings. This is a mistake, according to the integrationist, and for a very basic reason: there just are no context-free meanings. More generally, there are no context-free signs, either in speech or in any other form of communication. The proper name *Tony Blair* is no less context-dependent than the pronoun *he*. The adverbs *here* and *there* are no more context-dependent than the phrase *in Washington*.

The irony is that this pervasive context-dependence is concealed from us by our own readiness to supply the 'contextual' information required, according to the circumstances of the case. Thus we automatically assume that when a headline features the name *Tony Blair* this must be the current British Prime Minister. There are or have been thousands of other bearers of that name, but we rule them out of the reckoning because, in these circumstances, we do not recognize them as plausible contenders for the role. By the same token we assume that *Washington* must here be the American capital city of that name, that *U.S.* must be an abbreviation for *United States*, not *Upper Silesia*, and so on. All these assumptions doubtless dovetail to form a coherent hypothesis about the interpretation. But that coherence is itself a matter of contextualization, and is based on our familiarity with the kind of information that makes newspaper headlines. In all of this there is no basis for drawing a distinction between context-free and context-bound meanings.

Once we see through the speciousness of that distinction, we can also see how its rejection ties in with the integrationist assumption of indeterminacy of the linguistic sign. If the fixed-code doctrine is no longer accepted as a basic theoretical position, there is no good reason to accept any of its corollaries either. And that is just what the orthodox account of deixis is.

In order to allay possible misunderstandings on this point, perhaps it would be as well to restate what should already be evident. The integrationist has no interest in denying the difference between words like *me* and words like *John*. That would be obtuse. For if, in general, people were unable to grasp the distinction, they would presumably never be able to learn to speak at all (or else speech communication would be much more impoverished than we are accustomed to). The question at issue between the integrationist and the orthodox linguist concerns the explanation of that distinction.

According to the integrationist, it is quite misleading to try to explain the distinction in terms of 'contextual' factors, since all linguistic signs have to be contextualized in some way or other. The integrationist explanation appeals to the structure of the communication situation and the different ways in which it is possible for signs to integrate communicational activities. And here we come back once more to the integrationist principle of cotemporality.

What the principle of cotemporality says is that utterances make sense – or fail to make sense – in relation to what else is going on or has been going on at the time when they occur. The principle applies not only to language but to all forms of communication. Signs are contextualized in the first instance by temporal relations between events, as perceived by the participants. Communication does not stand outside the continuum of human experience.

Signs have as their basic function the integration of present, past and future. That is to say, they interrelate a present communication situation with previous communication situations and also, potentially, with future communication situations. There is indeed a macrosocial dimension to this: but it is misrepresented when we make the facile assumption that every time communication is successful this must be because it is underpinned by the existence of a fixed code which spans the temporal continuum.

Devices of the kind that traditional grammarians called 'tenses' do not occur in very simple communication systems: there is no need for them. And that is because the principle of cotemporality ensures that, all other things being equal, the sign will be taken as having immediate signification, i.e. reference to the current situation. Tense and similar features are devices of **'mediated signification'**, which use features of the current situation as a basis for focussing attention on some past or future situation.

A simple and familiar example of communication which involves no mediated signification is the way the British macrosocial system of traffic lights operates. There the signal remains in force for just as long as the appropriate colour or combination of colours is displayed. The red signal might be described as meaning 'stop now'. It relates to the events of the moment only. As soon as the red signal disappears, that message is out of date. If we apply the terms of traditional grammar to this case, it would count as a temporal deictic.

However, the traditional notion of deixis does not quite match the integrationist concept of immediate signification. To see this, consider how things would stand if the traffic light conventions were different. Suppose that when the light turned to red that indicated that the motorist had to stop not at this intersection but at the next one. In traditional terms that signal would still be a case of temporal deixis; but in integrational terms it would be an example of mediated signification. That is to say, a feature of the current situation would mean something with respect to a future situation – namely, what happens when you reach the next intersection.

Accepting the principle of cotemporality has many ramifications for semantics. For instance, it identifies one kind of nonsense. You cannot have a traffic sign convention that works retrospectively. In other words, the red light might mean 'stop now', or 'stop at the next intersection after this one', but what it could not mean is 'stop at last intersection you crossed'. It might, however, mean 'you should have stopped at the last intersection'. But that is precisely the difference between an instruction and an admonition. It explains why there are no languages with what traditional grammarians might have called 'past tense imperatives'.

The traffic lights example will also serve to illustrate two other important points in integrational semiology. The first is that the major difference between traffic-lights communication and speech communication in English is that the former is based on a fixed code whereas the latter is not. The great error of orthodox linguistics, as has been mentioned earlier, is to suppose that languages like English are just very complex fixed codes. This is to overlook a fundamental difference.

The traffic lights work on the basis of a small, fixed number of signals, and a very restricted inventory of possible 'messages'. That is part of the efficiency of the system. It would be counterproductive and potentially dangerous to operate traffic lights other than with a fairly simple fixed code. In the case of English, nothing could be further from the case. The ultimate reason for the indeterminacy of the linguistic sign is that speech communication has to be flexible enough to adapt to all kinds of unforeseen situations. If speech could not do that, then the history of the human race would probably have come to an end many millennia ago.

The traffic-lights code is designed to deal with one recurrent type of communication situation, and only one. It is recurrent because it is deliberately *made* to recur. It is a situation involving junctions or intersections in which the problem to be resolved is always that of giving temporary priority to one or more streams of traffic. In other words, the situation itself is already a set piece, designed artificially to facilitate road usage. If all communication situations were set pieces, then doubtless the human race would have evolved a whole series of fixed codes to deal with them.

But life is not a series of set pieces. It involves too much push and shove and too much give and take. That does not prevent human beings from instituting all kinds of macrosocial formalities and restrictions in an effort to establish order rather than chaos in human conduct. But these attempts are always impositions upon a basically open-ended, non-regulated flow of activities, in which individuals pursue their own goals in ways that are often mutually incompatible. *That* is the state of affairs language has to deal with. And until linguistic theory gives due recognition to that fundamental requirement, it is bound to produce linguistic analyses which falsify the way language actually operates in human affairs.

Cotemporality and linguistic facts

How does the integrational principle of cotemporality bear on the question 'What is a linguistic fact?' In various ways, both directly and indirectly. Let us go back to Hempel's example and consider a very simple claim of the kind that orthodox linguistics takes for granted as uncontroversial. For instance: 'there is an English word *hat*'. As far as the orthodox linguist is concerned that is simply a statement of linguistic fact. It is on a par with saying, 'On roads in Britain, one of the traffic signals is a red light.' But neither statement deals with any first-order communicational behaviour at all. What such statements formulate is, at best, an abstraction from the observer's study of an unspecified number of first-order episodes of communication.

Once we realize this, there is a temptation to suppose that the 'real' linguistic facts are not these macrosocial abstractions but the particular events which instantiate them. So we might suppose that, for instance, although 'there is an English word *hat*' does not state a linguistic fact, 'John uttered the English word *hat*' does. This would be like shifting in the traffic-lights case to describing a particular instance of a driver stopping for a particular red light at a particular junction. But this move does not quite fit the bill either, because in the linguistic case the previous abstraction about the English language already infiltrates this new statement: its presence is signalled by the phrase 'the English word *hat*'.

So there is then a temptation to get down to an even more concrete level of description and try 'John uttered the sounds [hat]'. Does that capture a linguistic fact? Well, clearly not, because John might not have been saying anything at all. Perhaps he was doing breathing exercises, or imitating the sound of the bellows in the local smithy, or reacting vocally to the ball that hit him sharply on the shin while he was dreaming at first slip. There might be a variety of 'non-linguistic' reasons why these particular sounds were made. So it seems that somewhere in between the last two statements the 'linguistic fact' has mysteriously disappeared.

This is one way of broaching a problem which has caused much vexation in modern linguistics: the relationship between 'phonetics' and 'phonology'. It is often claimed that the statements of the phonetician differ from those of the descriptive phonologist in just this respect: that the phonetician's statements do not state linguistic facts whereas the phonologist's do. Thus what you see on a sound spectrogram is no more than a picture of a rather complex acoustic disturbance. But when the phonologist comes along and identifies this as a pronunciation of the English word or syllable *hat*, then suddenly a linguistic fact has appeared. Possibly two or more linguistic facts, depending on how you count them.

If this is true, we are entitled to ask 'Where did the linguistic facts come from?' And the answer is 'The phonologist brought them into the laboratory; or, at least, what purport to be linguistics facts.' They were not there before. All we had before was the record of an acoustic disturbance registered by the microphone.

Even so, there is still something of a mystery here, because we do not know exactly where the phonologist got the linguistic facts from. And the answer is that it is the phonologist who constructs them. What purports to be phonological description is precisely that: a construction of 'linguistic facts', i.e. macrosocial abstractions. And that construction is usually based, as we have already seen, on the search for linguistic invariants – in this case the so-called 'phonemes' or whatever other units the phonologist is operating with.

Now there is a less respectful phrase than 'constructing linguistic facts', which is 'cooking them up'. And this takes us straight back to the 'hocus-pocus' controversy. But that was always a controversy between two wings of orthodox linguistics. A more interesting question to pursue for our present purposes is whether, when communication is viewed in an integrational perspective, there are any 'linguistic facts' at all.

The point was made earlier that for the integrationist there is no hard and fast line to be drawn between the linguistic and the non-linguistic features of communication. So the answer has to be 'no' if the identification of linguistic facts is construed as implying the adoption of some set of criteria for distinguishing them from non-linguistic facts. However, this does not mean that there are no facts of any kind in the communicational domain. It may simply mean that they are not the kind of facts that the phonologist cooks up.

What the God's-truth phonologist typically does is decontextualize certain acoustic disturbances and then claim to have found certain phonological units or patterns 'in the data'. They can be found because, allegedly, they were already there *in realia*. Jakobson and Halle (1956, p.8), for example, claim that 'the distinctive features are present in the sound waves'. Consequently all the linguist has to do is observe the sound waves carefully – provided, of course, that the linguist has a clear idea of what to look for. But this is presented as being no different in principle from, say, the botanist looking for plant specimens or the ornithologist looking for the great crested grebe. The claim is: we know they are there somewhere – it is only a question of looking hard enough.

What the hocus-pocus phonologist does is rather different. Given exactly the same evidence of acoustic disturbance, the hocus-pocus phonologist will say: 'Well, there are various ways this could be described, but I choose to describe it in terms of the following units, categories and assumptions. I think the advantages of describing it in this way are such-and-such, although I realize that things might look quite different if I chose another set.' There is no claim here that any of the resultant pattern is objectively 'in the data'. The exercise is simply one of systematic classification. That 'classifying' enterprise is explicitly rejected by Jakobson and Halle: they call it the 'generic' view of phonology, and dismiss it on various grounds, including failure to recognize that in the case of both phonemes and distinctive features 'we are primarily concerned with a constant which is present in the various particulars' (Jakobson and Halle, 1956, p.13). What they call a 'constant' is nothing other than what the integrationist calls an invariant; and the invariants Jakobson and Halle are looking for are deemed to be 'really there'. So it is not like the case of Diogenes looking for an honest man, but being prepared to admit that maybe there are no honest men to be found.

It is interesting that Jakobson later repudiated the whole hocus-pocus controversy. In 1962 (Jakobson, 1962, p.650) he wrote:

> the notorious linguistic controversy between the "hocus-pocus" position and the "God-given truth" is aimless. Any phonemic or grammatical opposition is neither fictional nor metaphysical, but simply and solely a CODE-GIVEN truth.

The substance of this claim depends, evidently, on what the 'code' is supposed to be, and Jakobson's answer is unequivocal: 'the verbal code is a real property of any speech community'. We are back to the classic fixed-code approach. In other words, Jakobson shows no sign of realizing that this rejection of the controversy is *in itself* a way of reasserting a 'God's-truth' position, i.e. reaffirming his own belief in the language myth.

Where does the integrationist stand here? Both the hocus-pocus phonologist and the God's-truth phonologist have at least one thing in common. They treat what the sound spectrogram shows as 'data'. Where they differ is on how to turn this piece of 'data' into a description of linguistic facts. The integrationist differs from both by rejecting *ab initio* the alleged 'data'. In other words, from the integrationist point of view, it is not only the linguistic facts that are being cooked up, but the evidence as well.

What this piece of 'data' consists of is a decontextualized abstraction from the totality of some speech event. The sound is removed from the temporal continuum in which it was originally embedded. It is then processed by machine and exhibited for analysis in a static and quasi-permanent visual form. In short, we are no longer dealing with first-order phenomena at all by the time the phonologist arrives on the scene, but with mechanical surrogates for them. It is not only the hocus-pocus phonologist who is engaged in hocus-pocus, but the God's-truth phonologist too. That is the irony of the situation. The debate between them is a case of pot calling kettle black. They are not arguing about linguistic facts at all, but about how to treat so-called 'data' which they have already substituted for any linguistic facts there might have been.

This is where the integrationist principle of cotemporality begins to bite as far as linguistic methodology is concerned. It rejects any attempt to remove evidence from its original setting; and this is because the result of any such removal is that the constitutive temporal pattern of integration is automatically obscured.

This is sometimes treated as a kind of 'observer paradox', but that is not quite what it is. The linguist can observe communication without necessarily interfering with it. But to observe it *qua* communication necessarily involves making some interpretation of it. The distortion the integrationist protests against is a distortion which arises not from observation, but, on the contrary, from one kind of interpretation, which involves treating an integrated whole as if it could be taken apart like a machine in order to isolate the ultimate constituents.

Axioms of integrational semiology

In language, there are no ultimate constituents. Saussure probably got as far as realizing this, and he may have been the first linguist in the history of the Western tradition to do so. But he was so disconcerted by the realization, and so conscious that it flew in the face of everything his fellow linguists believed, that he turned the realization inside out and declared that the apparent constituent units were features of the internal structure of one undivided and indivisible whole. He then had the problem of identifying this linguistic whole, and could do no better than postulate the familiar fixed code as the collective property of every speech community. That is why Saussure's thinking about language appears simultaneously so revolutionary and so traditional.

But if we reject Saussure's solution, where are linguistic facts – if there are any – to be found? The integrational answer to this follows directly from the principle of cotemporality and the two semiological axioms that it sponsors. These axioms state:

> 1. *What constitutes a sign is not given independently of the situation in which it occurs or of its material manifestation in that situation.*
> 2. *The value of a sign (i.e. its signification) is a function of the integrational proficiency which its identification and interpretation presuppose.* (Harris, 1996c, p.154)

If these axioms are accepted, it follows that the only facts an integrationist recognizes are those recognized in the communication situation by the participants themselves. But these, it should be noted, will correspond neither to the linguistic facts identified by the investigations of the orthodox linguist, nor to the so-called 'data' on which the investigations are supposedly based.

This may initially seem disconcerting; but it corresponds exactly to what we knew as lay participants long before any professional linguist arrived on the scene. It is a matter of everyday experience that situations arise in which we are called upon to establish the relevant 'linguistic facts', and we often do so in order that the communicational process may proceed without a hitch. We are asked to repeat, to clarify, to explain, to amplify, to agree or disagree, and so on. 'What was said' and 'what was meant' are variables constantly subject to monitoring by the participants themselves. Consider the following exchange:

Q. 'Did you say *bat*?'
A. 'No, I said *hat*.'

The point of raising this question is that the questioner is uncertain and seeks confirmation. But the confirmation is not about the existence of any English word, nor about the acoustic 'data'. It is about what the interlocutor said. The signs that occur in first-order communication are those that the participants construe as occurring, and what is signified is what the participants construe as having been signified. *There is no higher court of appeal.* The linguistic facts are facts which the participants have to establish to their own satisfaction. And they may not always be in agreement with one another about such matters. They have no other basis for establishing these facts than their own communicational proficiency – that is to say, their own experience in whatever forms of integration are involved. This applies as much to language as to any other form of communication.

A 'lay-oriented' linguistics

Communication between two people is always a form of reciprocal adjustment. And linguistic communication is no exception. Sometimes the outcome may be satisfactory to both parties. Sometimes it may be satisfactory to one but not to the other. Sometimes it may be satisfactory to neither. There are no guarantees in advance. It is this open-endedness that integrationists recognize as a fundamental property of the communication process.

The great error here would be to suppose that the phonologist's analysis of the acoustic 'data' as an utterance of the English sequence of phonemes /hat/ is a 'scientific' confirmation or translation into 'scientific' language of the participant's assertion 'I said *hat*.' Nothing could be more mistaken. If my interlocutor asks what I said and I reply 'I said *hat*' I am not proposing an analysis of the utterance: I am just repeating what I had previously said. By contrast, there is no way in which the phonologist's statement could pass for a repetition of anything.

In short, whenever there are linguistic facts available, it is the participants who are in possession of them. If a linguist wishes to have access to these facts, there is no option but to try to recover them from the participants. One of the greatest sources of confusion ever introduced into modern linguistics was the notion that the linguist, by employing the right professional techniques, can somehow bypass the muddles and uncertainties that might beset the lay speaker and establish 'real' linguistic facts that no one else – lacking the training of a linguist – is in a position to be aware of. Some linguists have claimed that linguistic facts are in the final analysis facts about mental processes buried so deep as to be 'far beyond the level of actual or even potential consciousness' (Chomsky, 1965, p.8). If this is so, it follows that no mere lay participant can ever be aware of them – unless and until enlightened by the professionals who allegedly 'understand' such processes and how to describe them.

The integrationist rejects from the outset all pretentious claims of this kind, which, apart from being flattering to the ego of the linguist, are strategic attempts to steer linguistics from the domain of social studies into that of the natural sciences. If such claims were taken seriously, the result would be to turn linguistics into an arcane discipline of no general interest whatsoever. As far as the integrationist is concerned, any linguistics worth having will be 'essentially lay-oriented' (Harris, 1981a, p. 90) and the facts it deals with will be facts of the kind that have to be dealt with in everyday linguistic communication by those who engage in it.

The business of integrational linguistics is not to be confused with neurophysiology, or speech pathology, or auditory phonetics, any more than watching cricket is to be confused with observing how bats are made or pitches laid. If the linguist wishes to study language, it is no use conflating from the outset what is essential with what is merely ancillary, even if indispensable. On the subject of what linguistics is *not*, Saussure showed far more sense than many of his successors, whatever reservations one might have about his views on *langue* and *parole*.

The participants in episodes of everyday communication know perfectly well what questions to ask if they are in doubt as to what the relevant 'linguistic facts' are. And they can ask these questions because – and only because – they are equipped with metalinguistic resources that enable them to do so. In orthodox linguistics, the study of lay metalanguage has been totally neglected. It has been recently taken up in an integrationist perspective, and the results confirm what might have been suspected about its complexity (Davis, H.G., 1997). There is a telling quotation from Wittgenstein that might serve as a motto for future research in this field.

> When I talk about language (words, sentences, etc.) I must speak the language of every day. Is this language somehow too coarse and material for what we want to say? Then how is another one to be constructed? – And how strange that we should be able to do anything at all with the one we have! (Wittgenstein, 1974, p.121).

What Wittgenstein is attacking here is the assumption made by many philosophers that language is to be discussed only at a level of abstraction which removes it from the actual contingencies of everyday discourse. So sentences like *Socrates is mortal* are somehow made to do duty as blackboard examples 'standing for' an actual utterance, or even a whole class of utterances that might be or might have been made. Whether Wittgenstein realized it or not, this criticism also strikes at the heart of orthodox linguistics, which operates in exactly the same way. What has happened in linguistics is even more germane to Wittgenstein's point, insofar as the linguist has in many cases simply appropriated the metalanguage of every day, and insisted on reinterpreting it in accordance with segregational theoretical assumptions. It would clearly be foolish to treat such reinterpretations as providing 'scientific' explications of lay metalinguistic concepts. But, more importantly, the attempt to provide such reinterpretations merely diverts attention from the urgent need for research into the way lay metalanguage articulates the second-order macrosocial abstractions that are called 'languages'.

Further reading

* Harris and Wolf, 1998, Part 6, 'Language and Society'
* On lay metalanguage: Davis, H.G., 1997

Questions for discussion

1. 'There is a very small vocabulary available to most people for talking about language.' (W. Labov) 'Both English and scientific linguistics as metalanguages are greatly lacking.' (E. Figueroa) What would an integrationist say about these metalinguistic judgments?
2. 'Taking the speech event as a starting point, one can either study the function the language used has for ongoing social interaction [...] or one can take the reverse point of view and attempt to see to what extent the (broadly social) factors present in the communication situation influence what is expressed linguistically.' (G. Sankoff) Why would an integrationist reject this as a programme for sociolinguistics?
3. 'In many multilingual societies the choice of one language over another has the same signification as the selection among lexical alternates in linguistically homogeneous societies.' (J.J. Gumperz) Why would an integrationist doubt this?

4. 'We may assume that every community has some shared beliefs about language and attitudes toward language.' (C.A. Ferguson) Why would an integrationist *not* make that assumption?

5. 'We are always, all of us, in some sense still learners of the language.' (A. McIntosh) How far would an integrationist agree with this?

Postscript

Samuel Butler once observed that 'it is as great an abuse of words to limit the word *language* to mere words written or spoken, as it would be to limit the idea of a locomotive to a railway engine.' The integrationist's sympathy with Butler's point will already be evident from the preceding chapters, where the notion that non-verbal activities are no less part of language than verbal activities has been stressed. This *Introduction to Integrational Linguistics* has introduced its subject mainly by way of comparison and contrast with another approach – orthodox (segregational) linguistics – which not only focusses on words but specifically on spoken words as the essential building-blocks of language.

This contrastive strategy takes advantage of the fact that orthodox linguistics is more likely to be already familiar to the majority of students. But it is a strategy with certain risks attached and it perhaps invites certain questions. Is integrational linguistics, then, an *alternative* to orthodox linguistics? Or does it merely point to the need for something extra to be *added* to the orthodox programme? Or, if neither of these is the case, what exactly *is* the relationship between integrational and orthodox linguistics?

Integrational linguistics certainly does not seek to supply alternative or better methods of achieving *the same goals* as orthodox linguistics; for, in the integrationist view, the main goals of orthodox linguistics, particularly with regard to the decontextualized description of 'languages' (their phonology, grammar, etc.), are in any case either misleadingly formulated or else impossible of fulfilment.

Nor, by the same token, does integrational linguistics merely seek to fill a lacuna that orthodox linguistics has overlooked.

What integrational linguistics attempts to provide is an alternative perspective on language and the whole process of linguistic inquiry. This includes, by definition, the kind of inquiry conducted under the aegis of orthodox linguistics. Consequently, it provides a basis on which orthodox linguistics can be subjected to critical scrutiny.

Does this apply the other way round? Does the orthodox position in turn provide a basis on which to subject the assumptions of integrationism to critical scrutiny?

Readers who have worked their way through the preceding chapters might like to treat this as a final 'question for discussion'.

References

Allen, M. (1997). *Smart Thinking. Skills for Critical Understanding and Writing*. Melbourne: Oxford University Press.

Austin, J.L. (1962). *How to do things with Words*. Oxford: Clarendon.

Baker, G.P. and Hacker, P.M.S. (1984). *Language, Sense and Nonsense*. Oxford: Blackwell.

Bloch, B. (1948). 'A set of postulates for phonemic analysis'. *Language* **24**, 3-46.

Bloomfield, L. (1935). *Language*. London: Allen & Unwin.

Bréal, M. (1897). *Essai de sémantique*. Paris: Hachette.

Calame-Griaule, G. (1987). *Ethnologie et langage. La parole chez les Dogon* (2nd ed.). Paris: Institut d'Ethnologie.

Cameron, D. (1995). *Verbal Hygiene*. London: Routledge.

Carnap, R. (1956). *Meaning and Necessity* (rev. ed.) Chicago: University of Chicago Press.

Chafe, W.L. (1970). *Meaning and the Structure of Language*. Chicago: University of Chicago Press.

Chomsky, N. (1959). 'A review of B.F. Skinner's Verbal Behavior'. *Language* **35:1**, 26-58.

Chomsky, N. (1965). *Aspects of the Theory of Syntax*. Cambridge, Mass.: MIT Press.

Chomsky, N. (1980). *Rules and Representations*. Oxford: Blackwell.

Chomsky, N. (1986). *Knowledge of Language*. New York: Praeger.

Coupland, N. and Giles, H. (Eds) (1988). 'Communicative accommodation: recent developments'. *Language & Communication* **8:3/4**, 175-327.

Crystal, D. (1980). *Introduction to Language Pathology*. London: Arnold.

Crystal, D. (1985). *What is Linguistics?* (4th ed.). London: Arnold.
Crystal, D. (1991). *A Dictionary of Linguistics and Phonetics* (3rd ed.). Oxford: Blackwell.
Davis, D.R. (1994). 'Teaching American English as a foreign language: an integrationist approach'. In: Hayhoe, M. and Parker, S. (Eds), *Who Owns English?*, Buckingham: Open University Press.
Davis, H.G. (1990). 'Introduction'. In: Davis and Taylor (1990).
Davis, H.G. (1997). 'Ordinary people's philosophy: comparing lay and professional metalinguistic knowledge'. *Language Sciences* **19:1**, 33-46.
Davis, H.G. (1998). 'What makes bad language bad?' In: Harris and Wolf (1998), Ch.20.
Davis, H.G. and Taylor, T.J. (Eds) (1990). *Redefining Linguistics.* London: Routledge.
Dawkins, R. (1976). *The Selfish Gene.* Oxford: Oxford University Press.
Devitt, M. and Sterelny, K. (1987). *Language and Reality. An Introduction to the Philosophy of Language.* Cambridge, Mass.: MIT Press.
Evans, G. and McDowell, J. (Eds) (1976). *Truth and Meaning.* Oxford: Clarendon.
Figueroa, E. (1994). *Sociolinguistic Metatheory.* Oxford: Pergamon.
Firth, J.R. (1957a). *Papers in Linguistics 1934-1951.* London: Oxford University Press.
Firth, J.R. (1957b). 'A synopsis of linguistic theory, 1930-1955'. In: Firth, J.R.(Ed.),*Studies in Linguistic Analysis.* Oxford: Blackwell.
Gelb, I.J. (1963). *A Study of Writing* (2nd ed.) Chicago: University of Chicago Press.
Grice, H.P. (1957). 'Meaning'. *Philosophical Review* **66**, 377-388.
Guinness, G. (1980). 'How much context? The problem of relevance in literary criticism.' In: Forastieri-Braschi, E., Guinness, G. and Morales, H.L. (Eds), *On Text and Context.* Puerto Rico: Editorial Universitaria, University of Puerto Rico.
Gumperz, J.J. (1982). *Discourse Strategies.* Cambridge: Cambridge University Press.
Harris, R. (1973). *Synonymy and Linguistic Analysis.* Oxford: Blackwell.
Harris, R. (1980). *The Language-Makers.* London: Duckworth.
Harris, R. (1981a). *The Language Myth.* London: Duckworth.
Harris, R. (1981b). 'Truth-conditional semantics and natural languages'. In: Hope, T.E. et al. (Eds), *Language, Meaning and Style: Essays in Memory of Stephen Ullmann.* Leeds: Leeds University Press.
Harris, R. (1987a). 'Language as social interaction: integrationalism versus segregationalism'. *Language Sciences* **9:2**, 131-143.
Harris, R. (1987b). *Reading Saussure.* London: Duckworth.
Harris, R. (1987c). *The Language Machine.* London: Duckworth.
Harris, R. (1992). 'On scientific method in linguistics'. In: Wolf (1992), Ch.1.

Harris, R. (1996a). *Signs of Writing*. London: Routledge.
Harris, R. (1996b). *The Language Connection*. Bristol: Thoemmes.
Harris, R. (1996c). *Signs, Language and Communication. Integrational and Segregational Approaches*. London: Routledge.
Harris, R. (1998a). 'Language as social interaction: integrationalism versus segregationalism'. In: Harris and Wolf (1998), Ch.1.
Harris, R. (1998b). 'The integrationist critique of orthodox linguistics'. In: Harris and Wolf (1998), Ch.2.
Harris, R. and Taylor, T.J. (1997). *Landmarks in Linguistic Thought 1. The Western Tradition from Socrates to Saussure* (2nd ed.). London: Routledge.
Harris, R. and Wolf, G. (Eds) (1998). *Integrational Linguistics: a First Reader*. Oxford: Pergamon.
Hempel, C.G. (1952). *Fundamentals of Concept Formation in Empirical Science*. Chicago: University of Chicago Press.
Hjelmslev, L. (1961). *Prolegomena to a Theory of Language*. Trans. F.J. Whitfield (rev. ed.). Madison: University of Wisconsin Press.
Hockett, C.F. (1958). *A Course in Modern Linguistics*. New York: Macmillan.
Hughes, A. and Trudgill, P. (1979). *English Accents and Dialects*. London: Arnold.
Hutton, C.M. (1990) *Abstraction and Instance. The Type-Token Relation in Linguistic Theory*. Oxford: Pergamon.
Hymes, D. (1974). *Foundations in Sociolinguistics*. London: Tavistock.
Jakobson, R. (1962). *Selected Writings, Vol. 1*. The Hague: Mouton.
Jakobson, R. and Halle, M. (1956). *Fundamentals of Language*. The Hague: Mouton.
Joachim, H.H. (1906). *The Nature of Truth*. Oxford: Clarendon.
Katz, J.J. (1966). *The Philosophy of Language*. New York: Harper & Row.
Katz, J.J. and Fodor J.A. (1963). 'The structure of a semantic theory'. *Language* **39:2**, 170-210.
Katz, J.J. and Postal, P.M. (1964). *An Integrated Theory of Linguistic Descriptions*. Cambridge, Mass.: MIT Press.
Komatsu, E. and Harris, R. (Eds) (1993). *F. de Saussure, Troisième Cours de Linguistique Générale (1910-1911)*. Oxford: Pergamon.
Labov, W. (1975). *What is a linguistic fact?* Lisse: Peter de Ridder.
Labov, W. (1994). *Principles of Linguistic Change. Vol.1*. Oxford: Blackwell.
Locke, J. (1706). *An Essay Concerning Human Understanding* (6th ed.). [Ed. A.C. Fraser, Oxford University Press, 1894. Repr. Dover, New York, 1959.]
Love, N. (1981). 'Making sense of Chomsky's revolution'. *Language & Communication* **1:2/3**, 275-287.
Love, N. (1984). 'Psycholinguistic structuralism and the polylect'. *Language & Communication* **4:3**, 225-240.

Love, N. (1988). 'The linguistic thought of J.R. Firth'. In: Harris, R. (Ed.), *Linguistic Thought in England 1914-1945*, Ch.7. London: Duckworth.

Love, N. (1997). 'Integrating Austin', *Language Sciences* **19:1**, 57-65.

Love, N. (1998). 'Integrating languages'. In: Harris and Wolf (1998), Ch.7.

Lyons, J. (1968). *Introduction to Theoretical Linguistics*. Cambridge: Cambridge University Press.

Lyons, J. (1970). 'Introduction'. In: Lyons, J. (Ed.), *New Horizons in Linguistics*. Harmondsworth: Penguin.

Malinowski, B. (1923). 'The problem of meaning in primitive languages'. In: Ogden, C.K. and Richards, I.A., *The Meaning of Meaning*. London: Routledge & Kegan Paul.

Malinowski, B. (1935). *Coral Gardens and Their Magic*. New York: American Book Co. [Repr. Dover, New York, 1978.]

Martinet, A. (1964). *Elements of General Linguistics*. Trans. E. Palmer. London: Faber & Faber.

Matthei, E. and Roeper, T. (1983). *Understanding and Producing Speech*. London: Fontana.

McDonough, R. (1993). 'Linguistic creativity'. In: Harré, R. and Harris, R. (Eds), *Linguistics and Philosophy. The Controversial Interface*. Oxford: Pergamon.

McGregor, G. (1986), 'The hearer as "listener judge": an interpretive sociolinguistic approach to utterance interpretation". In: McGregor, G. (Ed.), *Language for Hearers*, Ch.9. Oxford: Pergamon.

Morris, M. (1998). 'What problems? On learning to translate'. In: Harris and Wolf (1998), Ch.23.

Moulton, W.G. (1970). *A Linguistic Guide to Language Learning* (2nd ed.). Modern Language Association of America.

Mühlhäusler, P. (1982). 'Language and communicational efficiency: the case of Tok Pisin'. *Language & Communication* **2:2**, 105-121.

Müller, F.M. (1864). *Lectures on the Science of Language. Second Series*. London: Longman, Green, Longman, Roberts & Green.

Nida, E.A. (1949). *Morphology. The Descriptive Analysis of Words* (2nd ed.). Ann Arbor, University of Michigan Press.

O'Donnell, W.R. and Todd, L. (1980). *Variety in Contemporary English*. London: Allen & Unwin.

Ong, W.J. (1982). *Orality and Literacy*. London: Methuen.

Paikeday, T.M. (1985). *The Native Speaker is Dead!* Toronto: Paikeday.

Pateman, T. (1983). 'What is a language?'. *Language & Communication* **3:2**, 101-127.

Pinker, S. (1994). *The Language Instinct*. New York: Morrow.

Quine, W.V.O. (1961). 'The problem of meaning in linguistics'. In: Quine, W.V.O., *From a Logical Point of View* (2nd ed.). Cambridge, Mass.: Harvard University Press.

Quirk, R., Greenbaum, S., Leech, G. and Svartvik, J. (1972). *A Grammar of Contemporary English.* London: Longman.

Robins, R.H. (1971). 'The structure of language'. In: Minnis, N. (Ed.), *Linguistics at Large*, Ch.1. London: Gollancz.

Robins, R.H. (1989). *General Linguistics. An Introductory Survey* (4th ed.). London: Longman.

Russell, B. (1912). *The Problems of Philosophy.* London: Oxford University Press.

Saussure, F. de (1922). *Cours de linguistique générale* (2nd ed.). Paris: Payot. Trans. R. Harris, *Course in General Linguistics.* London: Duckworth, 1983.

Siertsema, B. (1965). *A Study of Glossematics* (2nd ed.). The Hague: Martinus Nijhoff.

Smith, N. and Wilson, D. (1979). *Modern Linguistics: The Results of Chomsky's Revolution.* Harmondsworth: Penguin.

Strawson, P.F. (1970). *Meaning and Truth.* Oxford: Clarendon.

Stross, B. (1974). 'Speaking of speaking: Tenejapa Tzeltal metalinguistics'. In: Bauman, R. and Sherzer, J. (Eds), *Explorations in the Ethnography of Speaking*, Ch.10. Cambridge: Cambridge University Press.

Tarski, A. (1944). 'The semantic conception of truth'. *Philosophy and Phenomenological Research* **4**, 341-375.

Taylor, T.J. (1998). 'Do you understand? Criteria of understanding in verbal interaction.' In: Harris and Wolf (1998), Ch.13.

Taylor, T.J. and Cameron, D. (1987). *Analysing Conversation. Rules and Units in the Structure of Talk.* Oxford: Pergamon.

Todd, L. (1974). *Pidgins and Creoles.* London: Routledge & Kegan Paul.

Toolan, M. (1990). 'Largely for against theory'. *Journal of Literary Semantics* **XIX:3**, 150-166.

Toolan, M. (1996). *Total Speech. An Integrational Linguistic Approach to Language.* Durham: Duke University Press.

Toolan, M. (1998). 'Analysing fictional dialogue'. In: Harris and Wolf (1998), Ch.14.

Ullmann, S. (1959). *The Principles of Semantics* (2nd ed.). Glasgow: Jackson.

Wittgenstein, L. (1953). *Philosophical Investigations.* Trans. G.E.M. Anscombe. Oxford: Blackwell.

Wittgenstein, L. (1974). *Philosophical Grammar.* Trans. A. Kenny. Oxford: Blackwell.

Wolf, G. (1989). 'Malinowski's "context of situation"'. *Language & Communication* **9:4**, 259-267.

Wolf, G. (Ed.) (1992). *New Perspectives in Linguistics.* New York: Garland.

Wolf, G. and Love N. (1993). 'Integrational linguistics: an introductory survey', *Actes du XVe Congrès International des Linguistes*, ed.

A. Crochetière, J-C. Boulanger and C. Ouellon, **1**, 313-320.
Sainte Foy: Presses de l'Université Laval.
Wolf, G., Bocquillon, M., de la Houssaye, D., Krzyek, P., Meyard, C. and
Philip, L. (1998). 'Pronouncing French names in New Orleans'. In:
Harris and Wolf (1998), Ch.24.

Index

accent	46, 48
foreign	130
addressee	93, 97
Alberti, L.B.	121
Allen, M	6
allophone	15
alphabet	8, 19, 110, 118, 120f., 123
IPA	118
Roman	120f.
analogy	89f.
Aristotle	33f., 89f.
assertion conditions	106
auditory sign	115
Austin, J.L.	91
Baker, G.P.	13, 30
behaviourism	32, 63f.
biomechanical factors	29f., 91, 99, 105, 113, 115f., 119, 121
blindness	115ff.
Bloch, B.	45
Bloomfield, L.	10, 32, 39, 63f., 67, 73, 110, 131
Braille, L.	115
braille writing	115, 117
Bréal, M.	7, 63
Butler, S.	149

Calame-Griaule, G.	27
Cameron, D.	48, 62, 108
Carnap, R.	134
Carroll, L.	73
ceramics	117
Chafe, W.L.	21, 34
channel	97
Chomsky, A.N.	59, 60f., 64, 146
circumstantial factors	29f., 49, 79, 83, 85, 90f., 99, 103, 105, 137f.
code	11, 20, 22, 32-8, 40-6, 48ff., 52, 56, 61, 68, 70f., 73, 76, 78-81, 84, 88ff., 101, 104ff., 115, 125, 128f., 131, 134f., 138ff., 143f.
fixed code	22, 32-8, 40-4, 46, 49, 52, 56, 61, 68, 70f., 73, 76, 78-81, 88ff., 101, 104ff., 115, 125, 128f., 131, 134f., 138ff., 143f.
codification	47, 56, 123
communication	4 *et passim*
face-to-face	12, 22
non-verbal	93, 105
proficiency	107, 145
reflexive	27
self-	29
sender-receiver model	20, 23, 28f.
telephonic	12, 29
theory of	10, 20, 34, 68, 111
traffic lights	27, 139f.
communication situation	11, 53, 130, 136, 138ff., 144
comparative philology	7
componential analysis	66
conjugation	8
constative	91
context	22f., 68, 93-108, 136
of culture	95f.
of experience	95
of situation	94-8
phonetic	95
context-bound	97, 137
context-dependent	88, 138
context-free	35, 68, 102, 105, 124, 136ff.
contextualization	23, 81f., 93, 97f., 100, 102, 104ff., 138f.
conventions	98
serial	95f.
conversation	105
'correctness'	127
cotemporality	81f., 98f., 105, 119, 122, 138ff., 143f.

co-text	95
Coupland, N	49
Crystal, D.	2, 16, 21, 93, 95, 136
Davis, D.R.	57, 125
Davis, H.G.	9, 17, 30, 53, 62, 125, 146f.
Dawkins, R.	72f.
deaf	122
declension	8
decontextualization	13, 22f., 54, 80f., 85f., 106, 123, 127, 142f.,149
definitions	72f.
stipulative	72f.
deixis	136-9
determinacy/indeterminacy	10, 22, 32-5, 41, 61, 68ff., 73, 76, 84-90, 94, 97, 101, 131-8, 140
misconceptions of	132f.
regulated	88
determiner	132
Devitt, M.	65
dialect	44-8, 75, 97, 129f., 133
dictionary	26, 28, 31, 47, 54, 56f., 66, 68ff., 74, 77f., 84-8, 91, 98, 123
discourse	78, 93-108
analysis	106
open-endedness of	105, 145
drawing	117,121ff.
epistemology	17
ethnic cleansing	53
etymology	69, 74
Evans, G.	66f.
experimental method	16
extra-linguistic	95
Figueroa, E.	95
Firth, J.R.	10, 50, 95-8, 100
Fodor, J.A.	64
form (vs. substance)	111f.
free variation	129, 133
functionalism	8

Gelb, I.J.   121
genre   97
gesture   119, 122
Giles, H.   49
glossematics   111-5
glossing practice   77f., 86
glottic identity   55, 57
grammar(s)   7, 8, 13, 16, 19, 26, 28, 31, 37, 47, 56f., 59f.,
                                64, 78, 132, 149
        modistic   33
grammaticality   13, 38f., 60, 126f., 132
Greenbaum, S.   132
Grice, H.P.   71
Guinness, G.   102f.
Gumperz, J.J.   97f.

Hacker, P.M.S.   13, 30
Halle, M.   142f.
Harris, R.   9f., 16, 30, 33, 35, 43, 50f., 56f., 62, 65, 67,
                                84, 89, 92, 102, 108, 124, 131f., 144, 146f.
Haüy, V.   115
Hempel, C.G.   134f., 137, 141
Hjelmslev, L.T.   111-4
Hockett, C.F.   64
homophony   114
homography   114
homonymy   73ff.
Hovelacque, A.   7
Hughes, A.   46ff.
Humpty-Dumpty(ism)   71, 72, 92
Hutton, C.M.   128
Huxley, T.H.   1
Hymes, D.   97

'ideal speaker-hearer'   12, 70, 72
idiolect   45, 48ff., 59f., 129, 135
illocutionary act   15
integration
        communication as   28f.
        of speech and writing   12, 116ff., 123
        of vocal and non-vocal 12
integrational semiology   140, 144
        axioms of   144
integrationism   1 et passim

intention   70-3, 92
intercomprehension   45
introspection   126f.
'intuitions'   126f.
invariant   35, 68, 79, 83, 85, 102, 128-31, 134, 142f.

Jakobson, R.   142f.
Joachim, H.H.   17

Katz, J.J.   21, 36f., 64
Komatsu, E.   51

Labov, W.   43, 126-9, 133ff.
language
    academies   31, 47, 89
    and education   6, 8, 20, 31, 48, 110, 116, 123, 127
    as innate   18
    ethnographic theory of 93
    faculty   3ff., 31
    interference   52
    language-name   55f., 58f.
    language-teaching   31, 47, 57, 125
    lay views of   14, 39, 45, 58
    'limits' of   134
    national languages   31, 34
    'primitive' languages   101, 107
    standard languages   46-9
    symbolic languages   134
language myth   31-61, 95, 102, 127, 129, 134, 143
langue   11, 22, 81, 90, 112, 129, 146
Leech, G.   132
lexeme   15, 28
liberal arts   7
linguistic acts   82
linguistic appropriateness   47
linguistic behaviour   53f., 57, 126, 131
linguistic category   132
linguistic change   42f., 75 see also linguistics, diachronic
linguistic choice   133
linguistic community   12, 38, 44, 48f., 51, 55f., 58, 65, 75, 79, 88,
                                       125
    'homogeneous'   12, 50, 60f., 72, 104
    preliterate   12, 78, 110, 123f.

linguistic 'competence'   11, 65
linguistic correctness   34
linguistic creativity   4, 41, 68, 91
linguistic 'data'   13, 16f., 39, 90, 96, 128ff., 143ff.
linguistic description   13, 16f., 25f., 36, 38, 44, 47, 48ff., 54, 57,
                               65, 74ff., 97, 100, 126, 128f., 141ff., 149
linguistic experience   125
linguistic expertise   15, 19f.
linguistic facts   14f., 17f., 39, 43, 46, 75f., 97, 125-47
linguistic form   13, 17, 20, 22, 35ff., 39, 43, 45, 47, 61, 63f.,
                               68, 73ff., 98, 101, 110, 113, 124, 131, 136
linguistic idealization   41, 60f.
linguistic informants   52, 126f.
linguistic inquiry   4, 14, 18f., 23-6, 30, 41, 82, 100, 150
linguistic jargon   28
linguistic knowledge   104, 127
linguistic legislation   53
linguistic observation   23ff., 40, 43, 48, 130
linguistic 'performance'   11, 53
linguistic responsibilities   4, 71
linguistic rights   31
linguistic rules   8, 13, 79, 101, 127, 132ff.
linguistic sign   21f., 32, 35, 53, 61, 68f., 81, 89, 131, 135,
                               138, 140
    arbitrariness of   32, 37, 69
    autonomy of   76
    indeterminacy of   131, 135f., 138, 140
    linearity of   110, 120
    theory of   110
linguistic stereotyping   57
linguistic structure   36
linguistic theory   3 et passim
linguistic variant   45, 60
linguistic variation   40, 44, 46, 48f., 61, 79, 128, 130
linguistic variety   44ff.
linguistics   1 et passim
    autonomy of   10
    diachronic   42ff., 46, 49
    ethnocentricity of   19, 57
    generative   8, 10, 36, 38, 53, 65
    'God's-truth'   16, 18, 51, 75, 142f.
    'hocus-pocus'   16ff., 43f., 49, 75, 126, 142
    'holy-pocus'   18
    integrational   1 et passim
    lay orientation of   146
    lay views of   15

methodology of	6, 10, 15, 16, 39, 51, 111, 143
pedagogic	47, 57
philosophy of	99
phonocentric	12
professionalism of	14f., 19, 28, 53, 76, 144, 146
'proper'	109, 130
'science' of	2, 4, 15, 16, 17, 18, 36, 41, 51, 56, 59, 63, 101, 106, 126, 147
segregational	*see* segregationism
synchronic	42ff., 46, 49, 65, 73ff., 100
systemic	8
text linguistics	80
'utopian'	12, 52, 72
literacy	12, 19f., 56, 77f., 85, 109-24
Livingstone, D.	103
Locke, J.	32ff., 88, 94, 106
logic	6, 34, 134
informal	6
Love, N.	19, 43, 53f., 60f., 91, 96, 100, 124
Lyons, J.	48, 132f.
macrosocial factors	29f., 49, 91, 99, 105, 125, 130, 133, 139, 140ff.
Malinowski, B.	10, 50, 93ff., 101
Martinet, A.	109f.
mathematical notation	111
Matthei, E.	21
McDonough, R.	98f.
McDowell, J.	66f.
McGregor, G.	98
meaning	7, 13, 22, 26, 28, 34-7, 39, 61, 63-92, 94, 98f., 101, 124, 131, 134f., 137f.
context-free	68, 124, 136ff.
dictionary	80
figurative	68
invariant	68, 79
literal	68, 89f.
multiple	73
referential	97
sentence	80
speaker's	80
utterance	80
vagueness of	135
'mentalese'	37, 71, 118

mentalism	32, 64
metalanguage	26ff., 42, 51, 55ff., 65f., 68f., 76, 91, 100ff., 107, 123, 127, 146f.
metaphor	68, 89f.
morpheme	15, 28, 35, 78, 97
morphology	7, 35, 64, 110
Morris, M.	125
motivation	73
Moulton, W.G.	21
Mühlhäusler, P.	127
Müller, F.M.	7, 15
music	111, 116, 118
notation	111
name	26, 28, 89f.
nationalism	31, 34
native speaker	52, 65f.
neurophysiology	146
Newton, I.	127
Nida, E.	109
non-linguistic	95f., 104, 109, 141f.
nonsense	139
non-standard	46
noun	8, 72, 74, 114, 132f.
observer paradox	144
O'Donnell, W.R.	47
Ong, W.J.	124
'ontological toughness'	51, 56
Paikeday, T.M.	52
painting	99ff., 117, 121
paralinguistics	80
parole	11, 53, 81, 90, 93, 146
parts of speech	4, 8, 16, 136
Pateman, T.	58
performative	91
philology	7
phoneme	15, 28, 35, 136, 142, 145
phonetics	7, 8, 36, 141f., 146
phonetic transcription	128
phonocentricity	96
phonology	8, 35ff., 45, 64, 110, 141ff., 145, 149

photography	99
pidgin	52
Pike, K.L.	10, 50
Pinker, S.	34, 37f., 94
Plato	123
polysemy	73ff., 114
positivism	39, 106, 128
Postal, P.M.	36f.
pragmatics	80
predicate	8
'prestige'	46f.
processing	117, 120-3
'psychological reality'	16f., 21, 44, 75, 128f.
'purity'	52
Quine, W.V.O.	66
Quirk, R.	132
reading	91, 104, 115-9
silent	116
'real world' knowledge	65, 67
recontextualization	54, 99, 105, 123
reflexivity	24-8, 30, 55, 70, 73f., 100, 107f., 123, 126
relevance theory	80
repetition	28, 82, 131, 145
Robins, R.H.	3, 18, 112
Roeper, T.	21
Russell, B.	17
Sanskrit	8
Sapir, E.	10, 50
Saussure, F. de	7, 8, 10, 16, 17, 21f., 24, 33f., 36ff., 42ff., 49, 51f, 56, 61, 63, 73, 75, 81, 95f., 110ff., 120, 128, 131, 144, 146
Schleicher, A.	7
science(s)	64, 131, 134 , 145f. *see also* linguistics
language of	134, 145
natural	146
philosophy of	134
scriptism	123
sculpture	117
second-order constructs	51, 53, 56f., 77, 147

segregationism   9, 10-14, 19-22, 26, 34f., 40, 43, 48-51, 53,
                         55, 57-60, 63-66, 68, 76ff., 82f., 88, 95, 97,
                         99, 102, 149
semantic description   65f., 76
semantic determinacy   68ff., 73, 76, 87, 90, 94, 101
semantic deviation   89
semantic indeterminacy   77, 84ff., 88
semantic invariant   85
semantic knowledge   65f., 76f., 80
semantic metalanguage   65
semantic regress   71
semantic rule   134
semantic theory   63, 71f., 77, 84
semantic transference   89f.
semantics   7, 35ff., 63-92, 139
    segregational   65f., 68, 76f.
sentence   8 *et passim*
setting   94, 97, 105, 143
Siertsema, B.   111f., 114
signification   32, 102, 139, 144f.
    immediate   139
    mediated   139
sign   10f., 21f., 32, 35, 53f. 61, 68f., 76, 79ff., 83,
                         88f., 102f., 110, 112, 115, 120, 122, 128,
                         131, 135f., 138ff., 144f.
    auditory   115
    autonomy of   76
    gestural   119, 122
    kinetic   122
    linguistic   *see* linguistic sign
    metasign   27
    visual   115
    written   115, 120, 122
sign languages   122
signifiant   22
signifié   22
slang   47, 69
Smith, N.   59f.
sociolinguistics   39, 46, 48, 97, 126, 127
    interactional   97
spectrogram   141, 143
speech   23 *et passim. See also* parole.
    'correct'   127
    ephemerality of   122
    facts of   96
speech accommodation   49

speech act   23, 80, 91, 97
    components of   97
speech community   97, 126, 129, 144
speech event   93, 95f., 131, 143
speech pathology   146
speech sequences   96
'speech circuit'   21, 34, 94
spelling   74, 112, 114
Stanley, H.   103
Sterelny, K.   65
Strawson, P.F.   71
Stross, B.   27, 30
structuralism   8
subject of sentence   8
surrogationalism   67
Svartvik, J.   132
swearing   47, 125
syllogism   134
synonymy   39, 66
syntax   7, 35ff., 46, 110

'talking heads' model   21f., 26, 61, 63, 93
Tarski, A.   66, 67
Taylor, T.J.   9, 33, 92, 105f., 108
telementation   22, 29, 32ff., 36, 38, 63, 92, 94, 96, 118, 135
tense   136, 139
text   96f., 102, 104, 117f.
thinking   29, 37
Todd, L.   47, 52
Toolan, M.   9, 14, 56, 68, 70, 90, 92, 102, 105
translation   37, 125
Trudgill, P.   46ff.
truth   17, 67f., 70, 72, 85, 134
types (vs. tokens)   102, 128

Uldall, H.J.   111f., 114
Ullmann, S.   74, 75
understanding   105ff., 118, 136
universal languages   33
usage   127, 133
utterance   102, 147

verb   8, 69, 108, 114, 136
verbal repertoire   97

visual sign   115

Waugh, E.   102ff.
Wilkins, J.   33
Wilson, D.   59f.
Wittgenstein, L.   98-101, 107, 146f.
Wolf, G.   9, 30, 53f., 62, 92, 94, 108, 124f., 147
word   5 *et passim*
word-formation   133
writing   12, 45, 50, 68, 74, 91, 93, 109-124, 136
    braille   115
    definition of   121
    forming phase   117, 120
    glottic   116ff., 123
    interpretation of   118
    processing of   117, 120ff.
    sky-writing   122
    spatial dimension of   116f., 120f.

Zamenhof, L.L.   33